Smalltalk V®: Practice and Experience

Wilf LaLonde

School of Computer Science
Carleton University
&
The Object People Inc.

John Pugh

School of Computer Science
Carleton University
&
The Object People Inc.

(*Smalltalk V: Practice and Experience* is based on articles originally appearing in the Journal of Object-Oriented Programming.)

PRENTICE HALL
Englewood Cliffs, New Jersey 07632

Library of Congress Cataloging-in-Publication Data

LaLonde, Wilf R.
Smalltalk/V: practice and experience / Wilf R. LaLonde,
John R. Pugh.
p. cm.
Includes index.
1. Object-oriented programming (Computer science)
2. Smalltalk/V (Computer program language) I. Pugh, John R.
II. Title. III. Title: Smalltalk/V.
QA76.64.L34 1994
005.13'3--dc 20
93-27008
CIP

Acquisitions editor: **MARCIA HORTON**
Production editor: **RICHARD DeLORENZO**
Copy editor: **BARBARA ZEIDERS**
Cover design: **DeLUCA DESIGN**
Production coordinator: **LINDA BEHRENS**
Editorial assistant: **DOLORES MARS**

Smalltalk V: Practice and Experience is based on articles orginally appearing in the Journal of Object-Oriented Programming.

Printed in the United States of America

10 9 8 7 6 5 4 3 2 1

ISBN 0-13-814039-1

Prentice-Hall International (UK) Limited, London
Prentice-Hall of Australia Pty. Limited, Sydney
Prentice-Hall Canada Inc., Toronto
Prentice-Hall Hispanoamericana, S.A., Mexico
Prentice-Hall of India Private Limited, New Delhi
Prentice-Hall of Japan, Inc., Tokyo
Simon & Schuster Asia Pte. Ltd., Singapore
Editora Prentice-Hall do Brasil, Ltda., Rio de Janeiro

Contents

Preface iv

1 Multiple Representations 1
2 Generalization: An Activity Promoted by Object-Oriented Languages 19
3 Disk Objects and Meta-Level Facilities 33
4 Film Loops and Primitive Animation 47
5 Windows, Panes, and Events 61
6 Taking the Pane out of Building Windows 81
7 Combining Modal and Non-modal Components to Build a Picture Viewer 103
8 Pluggable Tiling Panes 121
9 Fuzzy Sets and Line Plots 141
10 Dynamic Data Exchange 169

Index 184

Preface

Introduction

Our motivation to write this book came from the interest shown by readers of our Smalltalk Column which appears in each issue of the Journal of Object-Oriented Programming published by SIGS Publications. This book is a compendium of short case studies featuring object-oriented programming in Smalltalk. Each chapter is a revised and updated version of one of our columns and is intended to illustrate either an important notion, an interesting approach, a useful application, or a novel observation that will lead to a deeper understanding of the process of design and implementation in Smalltalk. In each case, corresponding code in Smalltalk/V for Windows is discussed in detail and provided on a diskette.

Book Organization

Each chapter is designed to be read as an isolated unit. In each case, a working knowledge of Smalltalk is assumed but specialized knowledge needed for that chapter is reviewed as needed. Specific design issues and programming tips encountered when implementing the application are identified, lessons learned are discussed and the wider application of the techniques explored. In brief, the chapters are concerned with

- the design of classes with multiple representations (binary trees are used to illustrate the approach),
- generalization as the process that leads to greater reusability (tries and sharable dictionaries are used in this case study),
- the use of meta-level facilities (the design of disk objects with transparent forwarding encapsulation facilities illustrate the features),
- the use of bitmaps and primitive animation (a simple film loop facility illustrates the notions),
- the underlying event system for windows (a word translation application is used to illustrate the basic windowing facilities),
- more sophisticated user interfaces using entry fields, radio buttons, and standalone scroll bars (building a checking account manager),
- combining modal and non-modal windows in addition to graph panes and list panes (a picture viewer is developed),
- designing new panes with specialized events (tiling panes are developed and used in the context of a simple game),
- designing extensions of sets for fuzzy logic along with associated line plotting facilities, and
- linking Smalltalk to Microsoft Word using dynamic data exchange.

Except for the chapter dealing with events, all other chapters can be read independently of the others making it convenient for short study sessions.

Who Should Read This Book

This book is intended for people who have at least an introductory knowledge of Smalltalk. But it doesn't preclude those who are already adept with the language. Indeed, the chapters should prove interesting to novices and experts alike.

The novice reader is likely to focus on understanding the approaches and techniques used while the more experienced will look for the more novel ideas to expand their ever growing expertise.

Although our aim is to provide the reader with a better understanding of Smalltalk's capabilities and potential, let's not forget that we also wish to entertain. We do hope that you will enjoy reading this book.

Full Source Code Included on Diskette

The full Smalltalk/V Windows source code for each chapter is included with the book. Readers can file in the sample code into their Smalltalk/V Windows image and run the example methods to support the chapter material. Readers are encouraged to modify the examples, use the source code as a starting point for more elaborate extensions and applications, or port the code to other Smalltalk platforms such as OS/2 and the Macintosh.

Acknowledgments

First, we would like to acknowledge the help of Rick Friedman and the staff at SIGS Publications and in particular Richard Weiner and others connected with the Journal of Object-Oriented Programming for providing us with a forum for disseminating some of our thoughts about programming in Smalltalk to a wider audience. Thanks to the readers of our columns, whose feedback and requests for source code and extensions provided the motivation for the book. There were many others at Carleton University and The Object People who provided us with ideas or inspiration for the case studies described in this book; to those who are not individually acknowledged within the text, we thank you. At Prentice Hall, our editor, Marcia Horton, and Production Editor, Rick DeLorenzo, provided support and patience in the development of the book. Finally, thanks to our families, for their love and understanding and for learning to cope with the unreasonable lifestyles of authors and columnists.

1

Multiple Representations

1.1 Introduction

By definition, all instances of a class in Smalltalk share a common representation. In most cases, this is entirely appropriate. However, there are situations where it makes sense for instances of the same class to have different representations. In this chapter, we discuss the design of classes with multiple representations. This issue is not something you normally want users of a class to worry about but it is of great interest to implementors. Aside from being a new design dimension, it can also lead to a gain in efficiency.

When developing algorithms and data types for inclusion in a common library, it is inevitable that we encounter the notion of multiple representations for relatively common data types; e.g., when discussing familiar data types such as trees (or lists), we speak of empty trees and non-empty trees. We certainly need to distinguish between them; we do not speak of the subtrees of an empty tree, for example. Figure 1.1 depicts a binary tree representing the expression (1 + (2 * 3)) and containing no fewer than six empty trees.

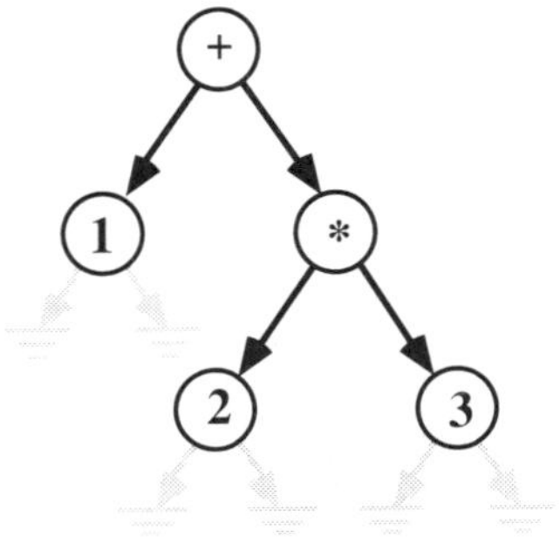

Figure 1.1 — An example binary tree.

The standard design for the class **BinaryTree** uses a common representation for all instances whether empty or not. Each instance has associated data and a left and right subtree but only non-empty trees need them. You might think of using **nil**, an instance of class **UndefinedObject**, to represent empty trees but this turns out to be a poor approach. For example, nil does not respond to the message **depth** nor does it make much sense to make it do so.

1.2 A Single Representation Design

In general, a binary tree is a structured collection of data objects. Hence a proper design should integrate binary trees with the existing collections; i.e., it should be defined somewhere in the collection hierarchy. For simplicity, however, we will make BinaryTree a subclass of Object and show only a subset of the message protocol. If we ignore issues related to representation and how to distinguish between empty and non-empty trees, most of the necessary design decisions are straightforward to resolve. For example:

- **Do we need to be able to print trees?**

  Yes, <'hi' -- <'there' <'you' -- --> -->> is an example of the notation we settled on.
- **What about store strings?**

  How about (BinaryTree label: 'hi' leftTree: (BinaryTree empty) rightTree: etc.)?
- **Do we need to define both = and ~=?**

  No, just =. Operation ~= is defined in terms of = and **not**.

- **Do we care about the semantics for copy?**

  Yes, we need to redefine both **shallowCopy** and **deepCopy** — the former makes a copy of the tree that shares the data elements, the latter copies the elements as well.
- **Should we design new control structures?**

  Yes, preorder, inorder, and postorder traversals on binary trees are well known control structures.
- **Do we need to worry about comparison operations?**

  Yes, equality for binary trees should take both the structure of the trees and the data into account. The default inherited from object defines equality as identity.
- **Do we need to be able to modify existing trees?**

  Yes, destructive operations like **leftTree**: and **rightTree**: would be useful.

Some design decisions require a little more care. We need some way of distinguishing empty trees from non-empty trees. An obvious, but naive, approach is to add another field to the representation, called **isEmpty** say, to distinguish the two cases. But this seems to be a waste of space.

A simple trick is preferable: use a non-tree in one of the subtree fields to indicate that the current tree is empty. By implication non-empty trees will be those whose subtrees are both binary trees (either empty or not). Hence we can think of an empty tree as an ill-formed non-empty tree. For simplicity, we will assume that a binary tree is empty if the left subtree is nil. This is convenient because uninitialized trees are automatically empty and, most important, users never need to be aware of this arrangement.

With respect to the class (as opposed to instance protocol), we can insist that Binary trees be created in one of two ways:

BinaryTree **empty**

Constructs a new empty binary tree and returns it.

BinaryTree **data**: anObject **leftTree**: aBinaryTree **rightTree**: aBinaryTree

Constructs a new non-empty binary tree with the information supplied and returns it.

One of the problems with this representation is what to do if someone attempts to add either data or a left or right subtree to an empty tree with expressions such as:

```
BinaryTree empty data: #testing
BinaryTree empty leftTree: aBinaryTree
BinaryTree empty rightTree: anotherBinaryTree
```

We could consider this to be an error. Alternatively we could automatically mutate the empty tree into a non-empty tree, an approach that might be described as more user tolerant.

A Smalltalk/V implementation of class BinaryTree using this common representation for all instances and using the above notion of automatic mutation is shown in Listing 1.1.

Note that the *depth* of a tree is defined to be the maximum number of nodes traversed from a root to a leaf; e.g., the tree in Figure 1.1 has depth 3 while an empty tree has depth 0. The size of a tree is the number of data elements it contains — 0 for an empty tree, 5 for the tree in Figure 1.1.

Listing 1.1 — Class BinaryTree (one representation version).

```
class name                                  BinaryTree
superclass                                  Object
instance variable names                     data leftTree rightTree

class methods

instance creation

empty
    ^super new

data: anObject leftTree: aBinaryTree rightTree: anotherBinaryTree
    ^super new
        data: anObject; leftTree: aBinaryTree; rightTree: anotherBinaryTree;
        yourself
new
    ^self error: 'trees are created with empty or data:leftTree:rightTree:'
```

examples

```
example1
    "Create a binary tree and see if it prints as
    <Hello <how -- --> <are <you -- --> -->>."
    ^BinaryTree
        data: #Hello
        leftTree: (BinaryTree
            data: #how
            leftTree: BinaryTree empty
            rightTree: BinaryTree empty)
        rightTree: (BinaryTree
            data: #are
            leftTree: (BinaryTree
                data: #you
                leftTree: BinaryTree empty
                rightTree: BinaryTree empty)
            rightTree: BinaryTree empty)
    "BinaryTree example1"

example2
    "See if the store string is correct for example1."
    ^self example1 storeString
    "BinaryTree example2"

example3
    "Construct an empty tree and have it mutate into non-empty tree <testing -- -->."
    ^self empty data: #testing
    "BinaryTree example3"

example4
    "Test depth which should be 3."
    ^self example1 depth
    "BinaryTree example4"

example5
    "Test size which should be 4."
    ^self example1 size
    "BinaryTree example5"

example6
    "Test = and copy; should return true."
    | aTree |
    aTree := self example1.
    ^aTree = aTree copy
    "BinaryTree example6"
```

```
example7
    "Test = again; should return false."
    | aTree |
    aTree := self example1.
    ^aTree = (aTree shallowCopy rightTree: BinaryTree empty)
    "BinaryTree example7"

example8
    "Try out the control structures; sum should be 10."
    | aTree sum |
    aTree := self example1.
    "First, modify the data fields to contain numeric data."
    aTree data: 1.
    aTree leftTree data: 2.
    aTree rightTree data: 3.
    aTree rightTree leftTree data: 4.
    "Next walk it, summing the information in the data fields."
    sum := 0.
    aTree inorderDo: [:data | sum := sum + data].
    ^sum
    "BinaryTree example8"
```

instance methods

querying

```
isEmpty
    "Special ill-structured binary trees with nil left subtrees are considered to be
    empty."
    ^leftTree isNil

isNonEmpty
    ^self isEmpty not

depth
    "The maximum distance between this tree and some subtree."
    self isEmpty
        ifTrue: [^0]
        ifFalse: [^1 + (self leftTree depth max: self rightTree depth)]

size
    "The number of data elements."
    self isEmpty
        ifTrue: [^0]
        ifFalse: [^1 + self leftTree size + self rightTree size]
```

accessing and modifying

```
data
    self privatelyCheckForEmptyTreeAccessingError.
    ^data

data: anObject
    self isEmpty
        ifTrue: [self privatelyMutateIntoNonEmptyTree data: anObject]
        ifFalse: [data := anObject]

leftTree
    self privatelyCheckForEmptyTreeAccessingError.
    ^leftTree

leftTree: aBinaryTree
    self privatelyCheckForABinaryTree: aBinaryTree.
    self isEmpty
        ifTrue: [self privatelyMutateIntoNonEmptyTree leftTree: aBinaryTree]
        ifFalse: [leftTree := aBinaryTree]

rightTree
    self privatelyCheckForEmptyTreeAccessingError.
    ^rightTree

rightTree: aBinaryTree
    self privatelyCheckForABinaryTree: aBinaryTree.
    self isEmpty
        ifTrue: [self privatelyMutateIntoNonEmptyTree rightTree: aBinaryTree]
        ifFalse: [rightTree := aBinaryTree]
```

comparing

```
= aBinaryTree
    "Two binary trees are equal if they have the same structure and equal data."
    (aBinaryTree isKindOf: BinaryTree) ifFalse: [^false].
    self isEmpty ifTrue: [^aBinaryTree isEmpty].
    aBinaryTree isEmpty ifTrue: [^false].
    self data = aBinaryTree data ifFalse: [^false].
    self leftTree = aBinaryTree leftTree ifFalse: [^false].
    ^self rightTree = aBinaryTree rightTree
```

copying

```
copy
    ^self shallowCopy
```

```
shallowCopy
    self isEmpty
        ifTrue: [^self class empty]
        ifFalse: [
            ^self class
                data: self data
                leftTree: self leftTree shallowCopy
                rightTree: self rightTree shallowCopy]

deepCopy
    self isEmpty
        ifTrue: [^self class empty]
        ifFalse: [
            ^self class
                data: self data shallowCopy
                leftTree: self leftTree deepCopy
                rightTree: self rightTree deepCopy]
```

sequencing

```
do: aBlock
    "Sequences through non-empty trees in preorder executing the block with the
    data."
    ^self inorderDo: aBlock

preorderDo: aBlock
    "Sequences through non-empty trees in preorder executing the block with the
    data."
    self isEmpty
        ifFalse: [
            aBlock value: self data.
            self leftTree preorderDo: aBlock.
            self rightTree preorderDo: aBlock]

inorderDo: aBlock
    "Sequences through non-empty trees in inorder executing the block with the data."
    self isEmpty
        ifFalse: [
            self leftTree inorderDo: aBlock.
            aBlock value: self data.
            self rightTree inorderDo: aBlock]
```

```
postorderDo: aBlock
    "Sequences through non-empty trees in postorder executing the block with the data."
    self isEmpty
        ifFalse: [
            self leftTree postorderDo: aBlock.
            self rightTree postorderDo: aBlock.
            aBlock value: self data]
```

printing

```
printOn: aStream
    "Empty trees print as '--'; non-empty trees print as '<data leftTree rightTree>'."
    self isEmpty
        ifTrue: [aStream nextPutAll: '--']
        ifFalse: [
            aStream
                nextPut: $<; print: self data;
                space; print: self leftTree;
                space; print: self rightTree; nextPut: $>]
storeOn: aStream
    "We can do better than the default."
    self isEmpty
        ifTrue: [aStream nextPutAll: '(BinaryTree empty)']
        ifFalse: [
            aStream
                nextPutAll: '(BinaryTree data: '; store: self data;
                nextPutAll: ' leftTree: '; store: self leftTree;
                nextPutAll: ' rightTree: '; store: self rightTree; nextPut: $)]
```

private

```
privatelyCheckForABinaryTree: anObject
    (anObject isKindOf: BinaryTree) ifFalse: [self error: 'using a non-tree as a tree']
privatelyCheckForEmptyTreeAccessingError
    self isEmpty ifTrue: [self error: 'illegal empty tree access attempted']
privatelyMutateIntoNonEmptyTree
    "For this implementation, empty trees have the same fields as non-empty trees.
    Hence it is easy to change one object into another object."
    leftTree := BinaryTree empty. "Now it's non-empty."
    rightTree := BinaryTree empty "Now its non-empty and well-formed."
```

1.3 A Multiple Representation Design

If you study the implementation of the class BinaryTree in Listing 1.1, you will notice that most of the code for the methods can be divided into two parts; what to do if the binary tree is empty and what to do if it is non-empty; e.g.,

```
self isEmpty
    ifTrue: [ ... ]
    ifFalse: [ ... ]
```

An alternative approach based on the idea of multiple representations which eliminates this kind of testing can be achieved if we create not one but three classes: **BinaryTree** and two subclasses **EmptyBinaryTree** and **NonEmptyBinaryTree** (see Figure 1.2). Class BinaryTree is designed to play the role of an abstract class. Empty binary trees are instances of EmptyBinaryTree and non-empty binary trees are instances of NonEmptyBinaryTree. Note that the new design is intended to work in exactly the same way as the old. Logically, we want users of binary trees to think in terms of the simpler design. This new design is purely an implementation technique to gain efficiency. The class **Boolean** adopts a similar technique with two subclasses **True** and **False**.

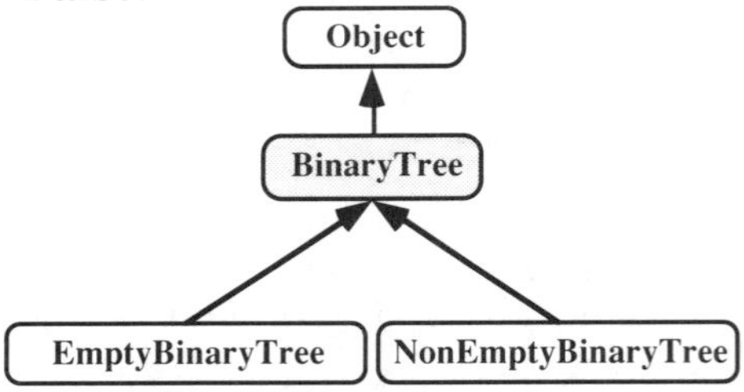

Figure 1.2 — The multiple representation BinaryTree hierarchy.

In this design, empty binary trees have no instance variables. Only non-empty binary trees have the data, leftTree, and rightTree fields. Almost all operations can be specialized for the two classes of trees. As shown in Listing 1.2, class BinaryTree contains the class methods for creating binary trees and any instance methods common to both subclasses. The example methods from the single representation version have not been included. Of course, if our claim that the use of multiple representations is transparent to users is correct, the same examples can be used without modification.

Listing 1.2 — Class BinaryTree (multiple representation version).

```
class name                    BinaryTree
superclass                    Object
instance variable names       "none"

class methods

instance creation

new
    ^self error: 'trees are created with empty or data:leftTree:rightTree:'
empty
    ^EmptyBinaryTree basicNew

data: anObject leftTree: aBinaryTree rightTree: anotherBinaryTree
    ^NonEmptyBinaryTree basicNew
        data: anObject; leftTree: aBinaryTree; rightTree: anotherBinaryTree;
        yourself

instance methods

querying

isNonEmpty
    ^self isEmpty not

copying

copy
    ^self shallowCopy

sequencing

do: aBlock
    "Sequences through non-empty trees in inorder executing the block with the data."
    ^self inorderDo: aBlock
```

The code in each of the methods for class **EmptyBinaryTree** (see Listing 1.3) and class NonEmptyBinaryTree (see Listing 1.4) was obtained from the corresponding code in the standard design by eliminating the **isEmpty** test and placing the true and false cases in the respective class. However there is a small problem. It is no longer possible to mutate an empty tree into a non-empty tree by initializing one of the fields. We have encountered the general object mutation problem: how to convert an arbitrary object (an instance of an empty tree in this case) to another arbitrary object (a new non-empty tree).

It is an interesting (and little known) feature of Smalltalk that any object can be mutated into any other. Object mutation can be used, for example, when a collection such as a set automatically grows to accommodate more elements. When a set is created, it only has space for a certain number of elements. To the user the set simply gets bigger when new elements are added. To the implementor, however, a new larger object must be created and initialized with the same elements as the original whenever space is exhausted. The difficult part of object mutation is that all references to the original object must be changed to refer to the new object. Smalltalk provides a powerful primitive operation, **become**: to perform this task. Intuitively, "A **become**: B" means "references to A are re-directed to B." The efficient implementation of **become**: and further applications of object mutation are interesting topics in themselves and will be discussed in more detail in Chapter 3.

Listing 1.3 — Class EmptyBinaryTree.

class name	EmptyBinaryTree
superclass	BinaryTree
instance variable names	"none"
comment	An empty binary tree is a binary tree with no data, left subtree, or right subtree.

instance methods

querying

isEmpty
```
    ^true
```

depth
```
    "The maximum distance between this tree and some subtree."
    ^0
```

size
```
    "The number of data elements."
    ^0
```

accessing and modifying

data
```
    self privatelySignalEmptyTreeAccessingError
```

data: anObject
```
    self privatelyMutateIntoNonEmptyTree data: anObject
```

```
leftTree
    self privatelySignalEmptyTreeAccessingError

leftTree: aBinaryTree
    self privatelyMutateIntoNonEmptyTree leftTree: aBinaryTree

rightTree
    self privatelySignalEmptyTreeAccessingError

rightTree: aBinaryTree
    self privatelyMutateIntoNonEmptyTree rightTree: aBinaryTree

comparing

= aBinaryTree
    "Two binary trees are equal if they have the same structure and equal data."
    ^aBinaryTree isKindOf: EmptyBinaryTree

copying

shallowCopy
    ^self class empty

deepCopy
    ^self shallowCopy

sequencing

preorderDo: aBlock
    "Nothing to do in this case."

inorderDo: aBlock
    "Nothing to do in this case."

postorderDo: aBlock
    "Nothing to do in this case."

printing

printOn: aStream
    "Empty trees print as '--'."
    aStream nextPutAll: '--'

storeOn: aStream
    "We can do better than the default."
    aStream nextPutAll: '(BinaryTree empty)'

private

privatelyMutateIntoNonEmptyTree
    "For this implementation, empty trees are completely different from non-empty
    trees. Hence a become: operation must be used."
    self become: (BinaryTree
        data: nil leftTree: BinaryTree empty rightTree: BinaryTree empty)
```

```
privatelySignalEmptyTreeAccessingError
    self error: 'illegal empty tree access attempted'
```

In this new design, non-empty trees have almost no error checking code. This is an important consideration since we expect many trees to be non-empty.

Listing 1.4 — Class NonEmptyBinaryTree.

class name	NonEmptyBinaryTree
superclass	BinaryTree
instance variable names	data leftTree rightTree
comment	A non-empty binary tree is a binary tree with data, a left subtree, and right subtree.

```
instance methods

querying

isEmpty
    ^false

depth
    "The maximum distance between this tree and some subtree."
    ^1 + (self leftTree depth max: self rightTree depth)

size
    "The number of data elements."
    ^1 + self leftTree size + self rightTree size

accessing and modifying

data
    ^data

data: anObject
    data := anObject

leftTree
    ^leftTree

leftTree: aBinaryTree
    self privatelyCheckForABinaryTree: aBinaryTree.
    leftTree := aBinaryTree

rightTree
    ^rightTree

rightTree: aBinaryTree
    self privatelyCheckForABinaryTree: aBinaryTree.
    rightTree := aBinaryTree
```

comparing

```
= aBinaryTree
    "Two binary trees are equal if they have the same structure and equal data."
    (aBinaryTree isKindOf: NonEmptyBinaryTree) ifFalse: [^false].
    self data = aBinaryTree data ifFalse: [^false].
    self leftTree = aBinaryTree leftTree ifFalse: [^false].
    ^self rightTree = aBinaryTree rightTree
```

copying

```
deepCopy
    ^self class
        data: self data shallowCopy
        leftTree: self leftTree deepCopy
        rightTree: self rightTree deepCopy

shallowCopy
    ^self class
        data: self data
        leftTree: self leftTree shallowCopy
        rightTree: self rightTree shallowCopy
```

sequencing

```
preorderDo: aBlock
    "Sequences through non-empty trees in preorder executing the block with the
    data."
    aBlock value: self data.
    self leftTree preorderDo: aBlock.
    self rightTree preorderDo: aBlock

inorderDo: aBlock
    "Sequences through non-empty trees in inorder executing the block with the data."
    self leftTree inorderDo: aBlock.
    aBlock value: self data.
    self rightTree inorderDo: aBlock

postorderDo: aBlock
    "Sequences through non-empty trees in postorder executing the block with the data."
    self leftTree postorderDo: aBlock.
    self rightTree postorderDo: aBlock.
    aBlock value: self data
```

printing

```
printOn: aStream
    "Non-empty trees print as '<data leftTree rightTree>'."
    aStream
        nextPut: $<; print: self data;
        space; print: self leftTree;
        space; print: self rightTree; nextPut: $>

storeOn: aStream
    "We can do better than the default."
    aStream
        nextPutAll: '(BinaryTree data: '; store: self data;
        nextPutAll: ' leftTree: '; store: self leftTree;
        nextPutAll: ' rightTree: '; store: self rightTree; nextPut: $)
```

private

```
privatelyCheckForABinaryTree: anObject
    (anObject isKindOf: BinaryTree)
        ifFalse: [self error: 'attempting to use a non-tree as a tree']
```

1.4 Extensions to Smalltalk/V

Throughout the implementation of the binary tree classes, **printOn:** methods have made use of a **print:** method on WriteStreams. This method is not found in the standard Smalltalk/V image but can be easily added as shown in Listing 1.5. Addition of this method (and a similar method **store:**) allows convenient cascading in **printOn:** and **storeOn:** methods. For example, the **printOn:** method in class NonEmptyBinaryTree was implemented as follows:

```
printOn: aStream
    "Non-empty trees print as '<data leftTree rightTree>'."
    aStream
        nextPut: $<; print: self data;
        space; print: self leftTree;
        space; print: self rightTree; nextPut: $>
```

A more common but cumbersome implementation without cascading would have been as follows:

```
printOn: aStream
    "Non-empty trees print as '<data leftTree rightTree>'."
    aStream nextPut: $<.
    self data printOn: aStream.  aStream space.
    self leftTree printOn: aStream.  aStream space.
    self rightTree printOn: aStream.
    aStream nextPut: $>
```

Because **print**: and **store**: are missing from streams, it is tempting to use the following alternative implementation with cascading:

```
printOn: aStream
    "Non-empty trees print as '<data leftTree rightTree>'."
    aStream
        nextPut: $<; nextPutAll: self data printString;
        space; nextPutAll: self leftTree printString;
        space; nextPutAll: self rightTree printString; nextPut: $>
```

However, the repeated use of "aStream **nextPutAll**: anObject **printString**" to append items to a stream is extremely inefficient. Aside from the fact that each invocation of "anObject **printString**" causes a new stream to be created, the most obvious source of inefficiency comes from the fact that the item to be printed is copied three times!!! Let's see why by considering

```
aStream nextPutAll: self data printString.
```

in the context of method **printString** for which one implementation is shown below:

```
printString
    "Obtain a printable representation of the receiver."
    | temporaryStream |
    temporaryStream:= ReadStream on: (String new: 16).
    self printOn: temporaryStream.
    ^temporaryStream contents
```

First, the **printString** method causes a new stream to be created — "temporaryStream". Next, the receiver "data" is asked to print itself on "temporaryStream" — this is the first copy. Then the **printString** method requests and returns the entire contents of "temporaryStream" — this is the second copy. Finally, this result string is passed to "aStream" as a parameter to **nextPutAll**: which copies it into the receiver "aStream" — the third copy. Clearly, messages of the form "aStream **nextPutAll**: anObject **printString**", when used, should be intended only as temporary code.

Listing 1.5 — Class WriteStream (extensions).

```
class name                                    WriteStream

instance methods

printing

print: anObject
    "Have anObject print itself on the receiver."
    anObject printOn: self

store: anObject
    "Have anObject store itself on the receiver."
    anObject storeOn: self
```

1.5 Conclusions

In this chapter, we have examined the use of multiple representations as a useful design technique in cases where different instances of the same class should have different representations. Smalltalk, like most other object-oriented languages, requires that all instances of a class have the same representation. However, the effect of multiple representations can be achieved by converting the desired class into an abstract class and introducing new subclasses for each different representation required. It is important to note that this is a technique for implementors — users need not (and should not) be aware of the use of multiple representations.

Self [1], an advanced object-oriented language based on the notion of prototypes rather than classes, more naturally allows the use of multiple representations.

As a side-effect of the discussion, we discovered the need to be able to mutate one object into another; a facility unique to Smalltalk and provided by the **become**: operation. This powerful notion will be the subject of further discussion in chapter 3.

1.6 References

1. Ungar, D., and Smith, R.B., SELF: The Power of Simplicity, Proc. of ACM OOPSLA Conference, pp. 227-241, Orlando, Florida, 1987.

2

Generalization: An Activity Promoted By Object-Oriented Languages

2.1 Introduction

Few programming languages have the power to induce generalizations on the part of the programmer. For example, after implementing a new data type in a traditional language like Pascal, we often gleam with satisfaction at the elegance, beauty, and efficiency of the approach. Then we go on to other things. We're done!!!

In a more powerful language like Smalltalk, your work is never done. It's actually dangerous to show it to anyone because the result is usually a suggestion that begins with "why don't you …" and contains other commentary like "… why restrict ..." among others. The process that is playing a role here is **generalization** — the art of removing restrictions to make something more useful; i.e., more **reusable**. Some trivial examples include generalizing small integers to integers by removing the restriction on the range of values supported by the former, generalizing array subscripts from integers to arbitrary objects to get what Smalltalk calls a dictionary, or eliminating the restriction that sets cannot have **nil** as an element (this is peculiar to Smalltalk). In this chapter, we will consider the problem of generalizing at the level of an individual class. This is an important issue that contributes greatly to the achievement of one of the goals of object-oriented programming — reusable classes.

To get a better feel for this notion of generalization, we will consider the design of a simple but well-known data type like a trie. The word trie is extracted from the letters in the middle of *re**trie**val* and is pronounced *try*. Unlike a normal search tree where the keys (strings say) are stored in the nodes of the tree, a **trie** is a search tree that typically uses the successive characters in a key to direct the branching to the data; i.e., the key is decomposed vertically and the components are used to trace a path from the root to a node lower down (typically a leaf) where the data resides. For example, consider the trie of Figure 2.1 (data not shown). Three keys were used, 'he', 'him', and 'ho'.

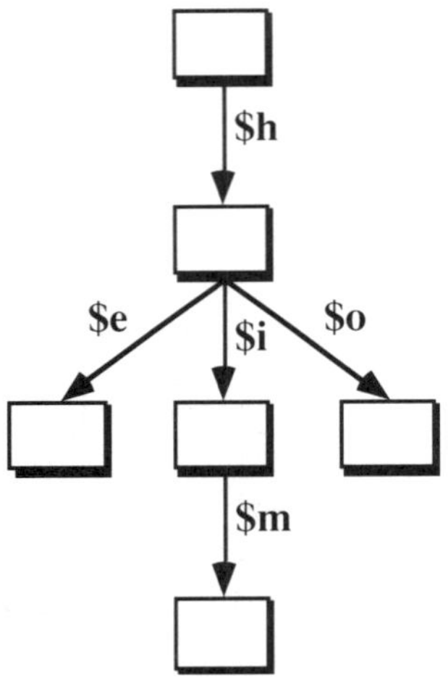

Figure 2.1 — An example trie.

The example in Figure 2.1 illustrates a trie in which the key is decomposed into its constituent characters. An alternative is to decompose it further into its constituent bits, in which case, the resulting trie is often called a **digital trie**.

A key property of tries is that trie entries beginning with a certain prefix are to be found in the subtrie for which the components of the prefix form the search path. For a trie with strings as keys, this means that all keys beginning with a certain prefix are grouped into a subtrie. Tries are therefore useful for applications such a spelling checkers where it is important to find incorrect spellings as quickly as those that are correct. Other applications might be a *thesaurus* where synonyms are associated with words or a *word completion facility* for disabled typists (or programmers); in this case, the system could automatically complete any word typed that has a unique prefix.

2.2 A Conventional Trie Design

To start the process, consider the following design based on an implementation from the ***Handbook of Algorithms and Data Structures*** [1], one of the few texts that provides both implementations and detailed analyses of algorithms. Since tries are search trees, the design is based on typical operations like **search**: and **insert**:. Both operations return tries rooted at the data insertion or retrieval points; i.e., after inserting a new string like 'his', data such as 'hers' can be associated with the returned trie by sending it a **data**: message. Alternatively, data can be retrieved by sending it a **data** message.

Listing 2.1 — Class Trie (class methods).

```
class name                          Trie
superclass                          Object
instance variable names             data subtries

class methods

instance creation

new
    ^super new initialize

examples

example1
    "Create a trie with 'hi', 'his', and 'ho' (insertion order is randomized)."
    ^Trie new insert: 'his'; insert: 'ho'; insert: 'hi'; yourself
    "Trie example1 inspect"
```

example2

```
"Create a trie with 'hi', 'his', and 'ho' (insertion order is randomized) and associate
some obvious data with them."
| aTrie |
aTrie := Trie new.
(aTrie insert: 'his') data: 'hers'.
(aTrie insert: 'ho') data: 'hum'.
(aTrie insert: 'hi') data: 'bye'.
^aTrie
"Trie example2 inspect"
```

example3

```
"Use the trie of the previous example and get the data associated with 'hi'."
^(Trie example2 search: 'hi') data
"Trie example3"
```

Executing **example2** results in the trie of Figure 2.2. The unspecified data values are **nil**. As designed, a search for 'hi' will return the trie containing 'bye'. Alternatively, a search for 'h' will return a trie containing **nil**. Since both cases return a trie, it is possible to update each one. On the other hand, a search for 'hill' will return **nil**, a non-trie indicating that neither 'hill' nor a longer word with prefix 'hill' are in the trie. This distinction might be useful for the *word completion facility* or *spelling checker*.

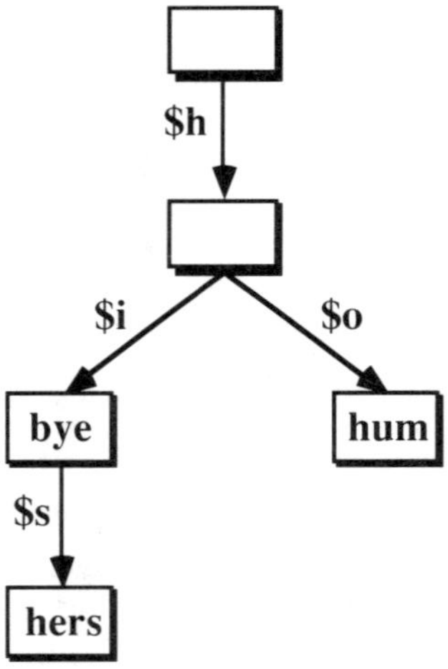

Figure 2.2 — A trie constructed by method **example2**.

The trie representation needs to keep track of only two things: (1) the data associated with the trie (field *data*) and (2) the tries lower down in the hierarchy (field *subtries*). Subtries are maintained in a dictionary indexed by the characters. Dictionaries are used instead of arrays for example because they are more convenient. For arrays to be used, we would have to map the characters to integers and use arrays that can contain the entire character set (or a printable subset if a suitable mapping was devised). Even smaller arrays could be used if we restricted the characters to lowercase alphabetics. But of course, the immediate reaction would be "shouldn't you generalize it to all characters."

Listing 2.2 — Class Trie (instance methods).

```
instance methods
instance initialization
initialize
    subtries := Dictionary new
data querying and modifying
data
    ^data
data: anObject
    data := anObject
inserting
insert: aString
    ^self privateInsert: aString atDepth: 1
retrieving
search: aString
    ^self search: aString ifAbsent: [nil]
search: aString ifAbsent: aBlock
    ^self privateSearch: aString atDepth: 1 ifAbsent: aBlock
```

private

```
privateInsert: aString atDepth: depth
    "Construct new tries on the way down unless one already exists. Returns the trie
    into which data can be added."
    | aCharacter newTrie |
    depth > aString size ifTrue: ["Found the string -- finished." ^self].
    aCharacter := aString at: depth.
    newTrie := subtries at: aCharacter
        ifAbsent: [subtries at: aCharacter put: Trie new].
    ^newTrie privateInsert: aString atDepth: depth + 1

privateSearch: aString atDepth: depth ifAbsent: aBlock
    "Returns the trie that contains the data for the given string if there is one;
    otherwise, returns the result of evaluating aBlock."
    | aCharacter newTrie |
    depth > aString size ifTrue: ["Found the string -- finished." ^self].
    aCharacter := aString at: depth.
    newTrie := subtries at: aCharacter ifAbsent: [^aBlock value].
    ^newTrie privateSearch: aString atDepth: depth + 1 ifAbsent: aBlock
```

All the work is done by the private recursive routines. They make use of an extra depth indicator to provide direct indexing to the associated character.

Now, the main thrust of our discussion has to do with generalization. How can we best generalize the design? Before we consider some possibilities, we might note that the design is already reasonably general. In particular, it permits arbitrary data to be stored in the tries. Of course, this isn't new to Smalltalk programmers but it is novel to programmers of traditional languages like Ada. Note also that it is possible to associate data with empty strings. Is this a fluke or were we clever enough to design it in? Now let's go on to new generalizations. Several ideas spring to mind: generalizing the associated values to permit **nil**, generalizing the key elements from characters to arbitrary objects, and generalizing the whole trie concept to a higher level data type.

2.3 Generalizing the Trie's Association Values

Recall that **nil** is not a valid element in a set; i.e., you can't add **nil** to a set. This restriction is unnecessary. Unfortunately, we designed in the same restriction in our trie. We can't associate **nil** with a string such as 'soup' because our design already uses **nil** to denote a non-existent entry in the trie.

To eliminate the restriction, we need a different technique for encoding non-existent entries. One way is to introduce a field called ***dataExists*** that is true only if an actual value has been associated with the corresponding field ***data***. Of course, this extra field is costly in terms of space. On the other hand, it is easy to provide the needed information without explicitly providing the field. The trick is to use some value other than **nil** that can't be provided by the user of tries; e.g., by binding ***data*** to the dictionary in ***subtries***; this assumes that ***subtries*** is never replaced by a new dictionary, which is the case in our design. It also relies on the fact that no protocol is provided for users to access ***subtries***. Listing 2.3 shows the changes required to accommodate this generalization.

Listing 2.3 — Class Trie (generalizing association values).

```
data querying and modifying
data
    ^self dataIfAbsent: [self error: 'no data exists']
data: anObject
    data := anObject
dataExists
    ^data ~~ subtries
dataIfAbsent: aBlock
    self dataExists ifTrue: [^data] ifFalse: [^aBlock value]
removeData
    data := subtries
```

2.4 Generalizing the Concept of Tries

To generalize the entire trie concept as provided above, it is necessary to consider tries from the perspective of the *user* rather than the *implementor*. What can we do with a trie? Intuitively, we take a string, place it in a trie, and then associate a value with it; i.e., it plays the role of a mapping mechanism. In particular, it maps strings to arbitrary values. Smalltalk experts will of course recognize this as a dictionary, more specifically a special case where the keys happen to be strings. From this viewpoint, a trie is a dictionary. If that is the case, then it should support the same protocol as dictionaries. In particular, it should support protocol such as **at**: and **at**:**put**:. For example, we might expect to be able to write the following:

```
aTrie at: 'his' put: 'hers'.
anObject := aTrie at: 'his'.
```

Unlike the **search**: and **insert**: protocol which return tries, **at**: and **at**:**put**: instead return the data inserted into the tries.

If a trie is a dictionary, is it simply a different implementation of the same thing? Why bother with tries at all if this is the case? Certainly, it might be worth distinguishing the two if there are significant space/time differences. If tries are significantly faster or smaller than dictionaries, why not replace the former and keep only the latter? Or, are there situations where tries are better and other situations where dictionaries (as currently implemented) are better? Dictionaries in particular currently use hashing techniques which are already very fast. Unfortunately, for general applications, this line of reasoning is probably a red herring.

A more important aspect can be highlighted if we again focus on the *user/implementation* level distinction. If a trie is a dictionary, there may be something unique about it that clearly establishes it as a special kind of dictionary — a **specialization**. We claim that a trie is a **sharable dictionary**; i.e., a dictionary that is decomposible into parts that are themselves dictionaries which can be manipulated independently. To be more specific, the **search**: routine returns a trie (a part of the whole) that can be used independently. This is useful, for example, to continue the search for additional associations whose keys have the same prefix.

Another point has to do with implementation technique. Does the view that tries are sharable dictionaries imply that Trie should be a subclass of Dictionary? The answer here is unequivocally **no**. We wish to view tries conceptually (or logically) as dictionaries but we cannot afford to make them inherit from dictionaries because we must avoid inheriting the representation used by dictionaries. Our implementation must therefore still inherit from Object or better still Collection (but we won't pursue this here). Consequently, all of the dictionary protocol must be added. We are not replacing the **search**: and **insert**: protocol but extending it with the **at**:, **at**:**ifAbsent**:, and **at**:**put**: protocol. Listing 2.4 shows the new implementation of class Trie with class methods **example4** and **example5** illustrating the use of the dictionary protocol.

Listing 2.4 — Class Trie (Tries as sharable dictionaries).

```
class name                    Trie
superclass                    Object
instance variable names       data subtries

class methods

instance creation

new
    ^super new initialize

examples

example4
    "Create a trie with 'hi', 'his', and 'ho' (insertion order is randomized) and associate
    some obvious data with it."
    ^Trie new
        at: 'his' put: 'hers';
        at: 'ho' put: 'hum';
        at: 'hi' put: 'bye';
        yourself.
    "Trie example4: Trie ('hi' -> 'bye' 'his' -> 'hers' 'ho' -> 'hum')"

example5
    "Use the trie of the previous example and get the data associated with 'hi'."
    ^Trie example4 at: 'hi'
    "Trie example5"

instance methods

instance initialization

initialize
    subtries := Dictionary new.
    self removeData

trie querying

isEmpty
    "As long as no data exists, must keep searching. Someone might have removed all
    data from the trie."
    self dataExists ifTrue: [^false].
    subtries do: [:aTrie | aTrie isEmpty ifFalse: [^false]].
    ^true
```

data querying and modifying

```
data
    ^self dataIfAbsent: [self error: 'no data exists']

data: anObject
    data := anObject

dataExists
    ^data ~~ subtries

dataIfAbsent: aBlock
    self dataExists ifTrue: [^data] ifFalse: [^aBlock value]

removeData
    data := subtries
```

inserting

```
at: aString put: anObject
    self privateInsert: anObject for: aString atDepth: 1.
    ^anObject

insert: aString
    "Obtain and return the trie into which nil is inserted and remove nil."
    ^(self privateInsert: nil for: aString atDepth: 1) removeData
```

retrieving

```
at: aString
    ^self at: aString ifAbsent: [self error: 'key not found']

at: aString ifAbsent: aBlock
    ^(self search: aString ifAbsent: [^aBlock value]) data

search: aString
    ^self search: aString ifAbsent: [self error: 'key not found']

search: aString ifAbsent: aBlock
    ^self privateSearchFor: aString atDepth: 1 ifAbsent: aBlock
```

printing

```
printOn: aStream
    aStream print: self class; nextPutAll: ' ('.
    self privatePrintOn: aStream for: ''.
    self isEmpty ifFalse: [aStream skip: -1].
    aStream nextPut: $)
```

```
private
privateInsert: anObject for: aString atDepth: depth
    "Construct new tries on the way down unless one already exists. Inserts anObject
    and returns the trie."
    | aCharacter newTrie |
    depth > aString size ifTrue: [data := anObject. ^self].
    aCharacter := aString at: depth.
    newTrie := subtries at: aCharacter ifAbsent: [subtries at: aCharacter put: Trie new].
    ^newTrie privateInsert: anObject for: aString atDepth: depth + 1
privateSearchFor: aString atDepth: depth ifAbsent: aBlock
    "Returns the trie associated with the string if there is one; otherwise, returns the
    result of evaluating aBlock."
    | aCharacter newTrie |
    depth > aString size ifTrue: [
        self dataExists ifTrue: [^self] ifFalse: [^aBlock value]].
    aCharacter := aString at: depth.
    newTrie := subtries at: aCharacter ifAbsent: [^aBlock value].
    ^newTrie privateSearchFor: aString atDepth: depth + 1 ifAbsent: aBlock
privatePrintOn: aStream for: aString
    | aCharacter aTrie |
    self dataExists ifTrue: [
        aStream print: aString; nextPutAll: ' -> '; print: data; space].
    subtries associationsDo: [:anAssociation |
        aCharacter := anAssociation key. aTrie := anAssociation value.
        aTrie privatePrintOn: aStream for: aString, (String with: aCharacter)]
```

Except for the data querying and modification methods, most of the instance methods shown in Listing 2.4 either have slight modifications or are new. Since the private routines for inserting and searching return tries, the **at:**, **at:ifAbsent:**, and **at:put:** methods must do a bit more to return the data instead of the tries. Method **at:ifAbsent:**, for example, uses the **search:-ifAbsent:** method to obtain a trie and must then extract the data from the trie that it receives. However, there is a small complication. If the block is executed, the result returned might not be a trie (it could be anything at all). Hence a **data** message must not be sent to this result. To avoid this situation, we must provide [^aBlock **value**] as the last parameter to **search:ifAbsent:** rather than just aBlock. Thus when the block value is obtained, an exit from the **at:ifAbsent:** method occurs without sending the extra **data** message.

2.5 Generalizing the Trie Keys

A next step might be to generalize the keys, which are currently strings, to arbitrary objects. In practice, this means replacing strings by something more general like arrays. Permitting such a generalization, for example, would allow book titles to be used as keys for their authors. An example of the use of such tries is given here as example6, and Figure 2.3 is a graphical representation of trie produced by example6.

```
example6
    "Create a trie with keys which are strings and arrays"
    ^Trie new
        at: 'his' put: 'hers';
        at: 'ho' put: 'hum';
        at: 'hi' put: 'bye';
        at: #(How To Enjoy Writing) put: 'Janet and Isaac Asimov';
        yourself.
    "Trie example6"
```

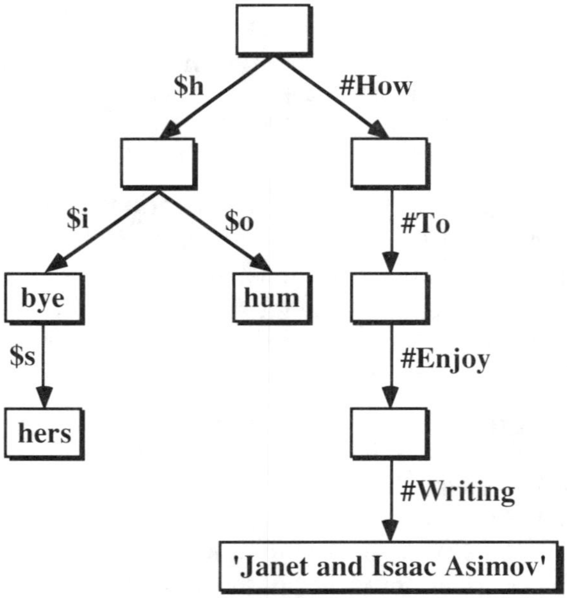

Figure 2.3 An example trie with arbitrary keys and values.

Naturally, there are other classes of collections other than arrays that would do just as well; e.g., ordered collections or even sorted collections. The natural question to ask is what subclasses of collections are suitable replacements for strings. Clearly, they are not all suitable. Sets, for example, will not do because ordering is important. Our implementation uses sequenceable collections — an abstract class for all of the suitable collections mentioned above.

To generalize the Trie class, we might ask if any work needs to be done other than changing parameter names from *aString* to *aSequenceableCollection*, for example? Will method **example4** from Listing 2.4 work as is? The answer is **no** and the reasons are simple. At least one semantic change is needed in method **printOn:**. Rather than create an initial key which is an empty string like '', we must, in the general case, create an empty sequenceable collection that is at least general enough to contain arbitrary objects — an array would do. Similarly, method **privatePrintOn:for:** must create a one element array for concatenation purposes.

We show a few methods in Listing 2.5 to illustrate the name changes in addition to the modified print routines.

Listing 2.5 — Class Trie (generalizing the Trie keys).

```
search: aSequenceableCollection
    ^self search: aSequenceableCollection ifAbsent: [self error: 'key not found']

printOn: aStream
    aStream print: self class; nextPutAll: ' ('.
    self privatePrintOn: aStream for: Array new.
    self isEmpty ifFalse: [aStream skip: -1].
    aStream nextPut: $)

privatePrintOn: aStream for: key
    | keyElement aTrie |
    self dataExists ifTrue: [
        aStream print: key; nextPutAll: ' -> '; print: data; space].
    subtries associationsDo: [:anAssociation |
        keyElement := anAssociation key. aTrie := anAssociation value.
        aTrie privatePrintOn: aStream for: key, (Array with: keyElement)]
```

If you study the final result, there are sure to be other extensions and generalizations. For example, there is no need to create a deep trie if there is only one path to specific data. Such variations are sometimes called **compressed tries**. The notion could be incorporated into the existing design or alternatively, provided via a subclass.

A small problem with the existing design is that the original keys are not kept. Consequently, insertions with keys that are alternatively strings, arrays of characters, and ordered collections of characters, for example, cannot be exactly recreated. This will only be a problem when the complete dictionary protocol is added because it includes sequencing operations like **keysDo**: and **associationsDo**: that provide access to the keys.

2.6 Conclusions

We have tried to indicate that the notion of generalization arises continuously in object-oriented systems such as Smalltalk because of the power of the language. Generalization can be viewed as a form of code polishing that strives to make the implementation more useful, more elegant, and less restrictive; i.e., more reusable.

Smalltalk allows the implementation of extremely generic data types — data types which permit generalizations that would be very difficult to achieve in other object-oriented languages. In fact, in our experience, after using Smalltalk for a period of time, programmers begin to consider generalization automatically and designs consequently improve. Indeed, it is seldom clear when the generalization activity is finished.

2.7 References

1. Gonnet, G. Handbook of algorithms and data structures in Pascal and C, 2nd Edition, Addison-Wesley, 1991.

3

Disk Objects and Meta-Level Facilities

3.1 Introduction

Smalltalk provides a few fundamental graphical data types; e.g., rectangles, pens, and bitmaps. In this chapter, we will extend their usefulness by considering the development of **disk bitmaps** — a variation of normal bitmaps that keep their associated data in a file. In the process, we will generalize disk bitmaps to disk objects and provide facilities for transforming disk objects back into the normal objects they represent. More specifically, disk objects will introduce us to transparent object mutation, meta-level facilities, and error handling. The concept of multiple representations discussed in Chapter 1 will be explored again in the context of disk objects.

The facilities that we are about to develop for transparent forwarding have a number of interesting applications that we will not pursue. For example, it can be used for "trapping" all messages to objects. This enables you to materialize the real object when needed (our goal here), to monitor messages and the accessing patterns of an object for debugging or history recording purposes, or to provide security to prevent unauthorized access. The approach is based on the notion of encapsulators introduced by Pascoe [1].

Although we are concerned with bitmaps, we will not need much knowledge about bitmaps themselves. As far as we are concerned, the following protocol is sufficient to allow us to get by:

```
aBitmap := Clipboard getBitmap
aBitmap displayAt: aPoint with: aPen "e.g., Display pen"
aBitmap release
```

Bitmaps are different from most other Smalltalk objects in that they must be released when they are no longer needed. The reason for this is that the bits are actually kept in operating system memory rather than Smalltalk memory. As a result, this space is not automatically garbage collected. Consequently, unreleased bitmaps ultimately cause operating system memory to be used up.

3.2 Bitmap Objects and Bitmap Libraries

As graphics becomes the norm in workstation technology, the requirement for pictures will grow. Some applications will use them as static pictures (or stills) and others will make use of them as part of animation segments. We can envisage large libraries of such pictures being kept. Only a small part of this library, however, is likely to be available in main memory — the majority will reside on disk.

This will be all the more evident when high quality color becomes an integral part of our workstations. To provide an idea of the space requirements, consider one 24-bit color picture on a 1024 by 1024 screen. The space requirement for one picture is 3*1024*1024 or 3 megabytes. Lower quality 8-bit pictures still require 1 megabyte. Lower resolution screens might divide these numbers by a factor of 2 or perhaps 4. Just displaying two seconds of high quality animation at 24 pictures per second would require 144 megabytes. It's easy to conjecture that 100 megabytes of main memory will be a minimum configuration for personal machines a decade from now.

In Smalltalk, pictures are instances of class **Bitmap**. With a large library of bitmaps, some facility will be needed to manage and distinguish between those bitmaps that are in main memory and those that are on disk. To support this, we might consider the notion of a **disk bitmap** — a variant of a bitmap in which the data resides in a file. Disk bitmaps might maintain a **file name**, an **offset** into the file, and a **size**. Alternatively, a file name and an offset might be sufficient if the size is kept in the file. This approach will permit many pictures to be stored in the same file (at different offsets).

3.3 Designing Disk Bitmaps

Should a disk bitmap have the same protocol as a normal bitmap; i.e., should we be able to use it as if it were a normal bitmap and have it take care of the discrepancy? It would be nice if that were the case because all software that currently works with normal bitmaps would then also work with disk bitmaps. How do we achieve this goal?

The obvious approach would have us define DiskBitmap as a subclass of Bitmap. But there are two problems with this approach: (1) the bitmap representation is no longer needed but the instance variables are automatically inherited anyway (we could, perhaps, set each instance variable to nil when they are no longer needed, but this is cumbersome), and (2) we need to override every single bitmap method, including those inherited through superclasses, to ensure that it pages the picture bits from disk as illustrated below for method **extent**.

```
extent
    self pageFromDiskIfNecessary.
    ^super extent
```

We can eliminate the first problem by designing disk bitmaps to inherit from Object. But we still have to implement every single bitmap method as shown above. Currently, the bitmap methods (in class Bitmap and in the classes above it in the hierarchy) total over 100 methods. Although this solution is technically feasible, it will be problematic when future changes to bitmaps are made as part of new releases. Every time a bitmap method is added or removed, a corresponding disk bitmap method would need to be added or removed. This is likely to become a major maintenance problem over the long run.

We need an entirely different approach. The ideal would be a disk bitmap that had very few methods — so few in fact that changes to bitmaps wouldn't have to be reflected in disk bitmaps. Could we in fact have no bitmap methods at all? But if we don't have any bitmap methods, how can we send a bitmap message like "**extent**" and expect the disk bitmap to work? Clearly, it won't work — a **doesNotUnderstand**: error message will be generated. That's the clue! Perhaps we can somehow tap into this message; i.e., provide an approach for handling the error which, in the process, can page the information from disk and re-transmit the original message to the object retrieved from disk.

But if we can make this work, what is the difference between, say, a disk bitmap, a disk set, or any kind of disk object? From the point of view of error processing, there is really no significant difference. Of course, the different kinds of objects must be stored differently. If we use store strings, for example, the difference won't matter because we can simply evaluate the store string to get the original object back — actually a copy of the original object. Ultimately, we should be able to store the information in a more efficient manner; e.g., using some kind of binary representation.

This suggests that we should generalize the notion of disk bitmaps to disk objects. Any object that has a corresponding store string (we'll generalize to a more efficient representation later) could be stored on disk and referenced by a disk object. Moreover, disk objects could be designed with a special property — the ability to transparently change or mutate into normal objects as soon as an arbitrary message is received.

Let's preview the basic idea: ensure that few messages are understood by disk objects and provide a **doesNotUnderstand**: method for handling all other messages. The task of method **doesNotUnderstand**: is to read in the required data from disk, construct a normal object equal to it, change the receiver into this object using the powerful **become**: operation (this was introduced in Chapter 1), and finally re-send the original message to the newly constructed object, and return the result.

3.4 Background for the Disk Object Design

To understand how this works, we need a quick review of the **perform** operations, class **Message**, the behavior of **doesNotUnderstand:**, and the **become:** operation.

First, let's consider the **perform** operations, a series of meta-level operations that can be used to execute arbitrary messages. For example, the following pairs are equivalent:

```
aString size
aString perform: #size withArguments: #()

1 + 2
1 perform: #+ withArguments: #(2)

anArray at: 10 put: 'home'
anArray perform: #at:put: withArguments: #(10 'home')
```

The family of perform operations includes variations where the number of parameters is fixed. For example, the above expressions could have been equivalently written as:

```
aString perform: #size
1 perform: #+ with: 2
anArray perform: #at:put: with: 10 with: 'home'
```

Next, consider what happens when an attempt is made to execute an illegal message such as

```
123456 copyFrom: 3 to: 5.
```

Since **copyFrom:to:** is not understood by integers, the system manufactures an instance of **Message** containing the selector **copyFrom:to:** and an argument array containing 3 and 5 and then sends the message "**doesNotUnderstand:** aMessage" to 123456.

The **doesNotUnderstand:** method inherited from **Object** displays an error message in an error window. However, we can write our own version, say in class Integer, that does something different. For the example above, we could re-send the message to a print string of the receiver. To do this, the specialized variation could be

```
doesNotUnderstand: aMessage
    | selector arguments |
    selector := aMessage selector.
    arguments := aMessage arguments.
    ^self printString perform: selector withArguments: arguments
```

This is clearly not the correct approach for this problem. We should implement **copyFrom:to:** in class Integer if it is deemed to be a useful operation. However, for disk objects, a more sophisticated version of this approach may be just what we need. More specifically, we want to mutate "disk objects" into "normal objects." The **become:** operation can be used as follows for that purpose.

```
object1 become: object2
```

The proper way to read this is to say "object1 is changed into object2." This happens quite literally. Every object that used to reference object1 in the system now references object2. Diagrammatically, the effects of the **become:** operation are shown in Figure 3.1.

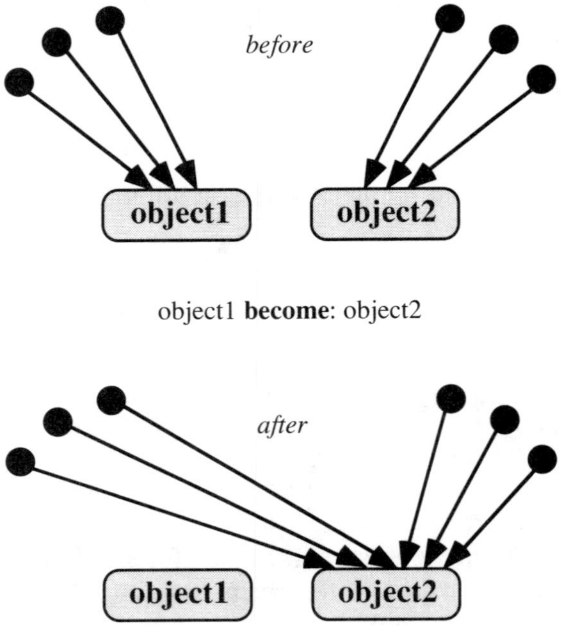

Figure 3.1 — Operation **become:** redirects references.

3.5 The Disk Object Implementation

Putting all of this together, we get the design shown in Listing 3.1. In an earlier design, objects were stored as store strings. To recreate an object, it was necessary to read in that portion of the file corresponding to the original object and ask the compiler to evaluate the resulting string. Consequently, the size of the string was needed in addition to an offset into the file. This size was stored as the first piece of information in the file. The design shown below makes use of the **object filer**, a special object called ObjectFiler, that is provided with the basic system. The object filer is capable of storing arbitrary objects in binary form rather than as a store string. It has its own private techniques for keeping track of the binary size of the object. Consequently, there is no need for a size to be stored. In the listings shown below, the code for both variations are provided but the code for the store strings is commented out.

Additionally, there are some extensions that are technically not needed but are useful for error recovery. For example, when a message is sent to a disk object that references a non-existent file, an error message is generated. The error notifier will typically provide a short stack of the last few messages and their receivers to users of the system. As a minimum, this will result in the message "class" being sent to the disk object which, of course, causes the same error message to result since the disk object will attempt to read itself from disk and mutate to respond to this "class" message. To detect this, we have added a "busy" instance variable which can be used to detect if a message is being sent to the disk object before it has completely processed an earlier message. For simplicity, we mutate into an identity dictionary containing the disk object's data so that further error messages are inhibited.

Once a "disk object" has mutated, messages send to the corresponding "normal object" are processed in the standard manner. If they are understood, execution proceeds normal. If they are not, a debugger appears as it always does for standard Smalltalk objects.

Listing 3.1 — Class DiskObject.

class name	DiskObject
superclass	nil
instance variables	filename offset busy

class methods

examples

```
example1
    "This example takes three separate bitmaps and converts them to three disk objects
    in a single file. The disk objects are then retrieved as bitmaps and displayed on the
    display. NOTE: the user must provide the three bitmaps by click-dragging when
    the cursor is changed into the crosshair."
    "DiskObject example1"
    | bitmap1 bitmap2 bitmap3 filename |
    filename := 'diskObj.ex1'.
    bitmap1 := Bitmap fromUser.
    bitmap1 offloadTo: filename executing: [bitmap1 release].
    bitmap2 := Bitmap fromUser.
    bitmap2 offloadTo: filename executing: [bitmap2 release].
    bitmap3 := Bitmap fromUser.
    bitmap3 offloadTo: filename executing: [bitmap3 release].
    "Now use them as if they were in main memory."
    bitmap1 displayAt: 50@0 with: Display pen; release.
    bitmap2 displayAt: 250@0 with: Display pen; release.
    bitmap3 displayAt: 450@0 with: Display pen; release.
    File remove: filename

example2: filename
    "This example takes a single bitmap stored in a file, creates a disk object
    corresponding to it, and displays it."
    "DiskObject example2: 'flagdata'."
    "DiskObject example2: 'loopdata'."
    | diskObject |
    (File exists: filename) ifFalse: [
        ^MessageBox
            message: 'The ''', filename, ''' file does not exist. ',
                'Please make sure it is in the current ',
                'working directory with the correct name.'].
    "Convert to a disk object, and use as a normal object."
    diskObject := DiskObject new
        diskObjectFileName: filename;
        diskObjectOffset: 0.
    diskObject displayAt: 50@50 with: Display pen; release
```

compatibility

aboutToSaveImage
"Private - Default code. Copied from Object for compatibility."

instance methods

compatibility

vmInterrupt: aSymbol
"Private - Process virtual machine interrupt."
Process **perform**: aSymbol.
^self

modifying

diskObjectFileName: aFileName
"Set the file name of the receiver."
filename := aFileName

diskObjectOffset: anInteger
"Set the file offset of the receiver."
offset := anInteger

mutation

become: anObject
"The receiver takes on the identity of anObject. All the objects of the system that referenced the receiver will now reference anObject."
<primitive: 72>
^self **primitiveFailed**

conversion

asNormalObject
"Answer the receiver as a normal object."
| normalObject aStream |
CursorManager **execute changeFor**: [
aStream := File **pathNameReadOnly**: filename.
aStream **position**: offset.
"START OF STORE STRING VERSION
size := aStream **getInteger**.
normalObject := Compiler **evaluate**: (aStream **next**: size).
END OF STORE STRING VERSION"
"START OF OBJECT FILER VERSION"
normalObject := ObjectFiler **loadFrom**: aStream.
"END OF OBJECT FILER VERSION"
aStream **close**].
^normalObject

error handling

```
doesNotUnderstand: aMessage
    "Mutate the receiver into a normal object and try the message again."
    busy isNil
        ifTrue: [
            busy := true.
            self become: self asNormalObject]
        ifFalse: [
            "Error in asNormalObject, need to do something more desperate."
            self become: (IdentityDictionary new
                at: #class put: #DiskObject;
                at: #filename put: filename;
                at: #offset put: offset;
                yourself)].
    ^self perform: aMessage selector withArguments: aMessage arguments
```

There are two interesting points about class **DiskObject**. First, why do we want the superclass to be **nil**? So that any message we send to a disk object will cause it to mutate. This includes messages inherited by all objects; e.g., messages such as

```
aDiskObject printString
aDiskObject inspect
aDiskObject = anotherDiskForm
aDiskObject copy
```

But, there is at least one message that slip through the net, however — message == because it is hard-wired to bypass method lookup. Can you think of any more?

The other important point is that message **become**: cannot be understood by disk objects if these in turn don't inherit from Object. So we have to copy the implementation of **become**: from Object. It turns out to be a very small method because it's a primitive; i.e., built-in to the system. For compatibility, we also have to copy class method **aboutToSaveImage** and instance method **vmInterrupt**: from class Object. The first message is sent to each class whenever an image is saved. Consequently, we have to implement it even though it does nothing. The second message is sent to the active receiver in the currently running window whenever the user interrupts the active window via a keyboard control-C.

3.6 A Note on Implementations of become:

Early Smalltalk implementations almost invariably used **object tables** (see Figure 3.2) to reference the objects. More specifically, objects were referenced via a small integer index into the object table and the table entry contained a larger pointer to the actual object. All references were therefore indirect through the table. In these systems, the **become**: operation simply changed a pointer value in the entry for the receiver.

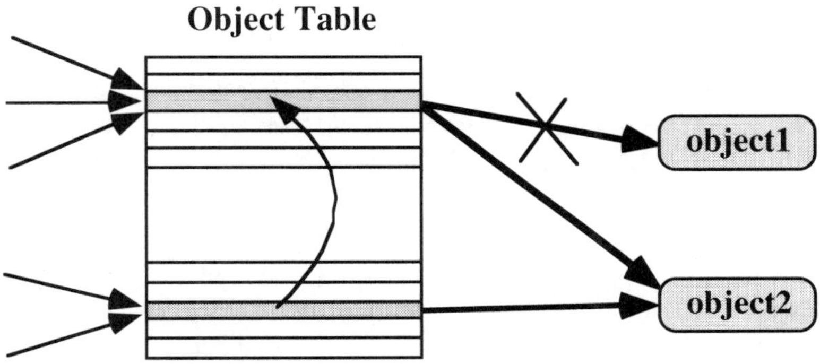

Figure 3.2 — Referencing objects through object tables.

Unfortunately, as the systems attempted to provide more and more objects, the indices grew to the point were there was no size difference between an index and a pointer. The advantage of the table became a disadvantage when compared to approaches using direct pointers in lieu of indices. On the other hand, implementing **become**: efficiently using direct pointers is more difficult. The naive approach makes an entire pass over all of memory and changes all pointers referencing the receiver of the **become**: operation.

An alternative is to copy the receiver to a new area and replace the original by a special **indirection object** (see Figure 3.3) that is invisible to the user. The Smalltalk run-time system can then indirect through these objects much as the older Smalltalk systems used to indirect through the object tables. The garbage collector can then be modified so that whenever a pointer to an indirection object is seen, it is replaced by a direct pointer. Over time, the indirection objects disappear eliminating the inefficiency of indirections.

One problem with this approach is that additional tests must be retrofitted pervasively into the interpreter or compiled code; i.e., almost everywhere

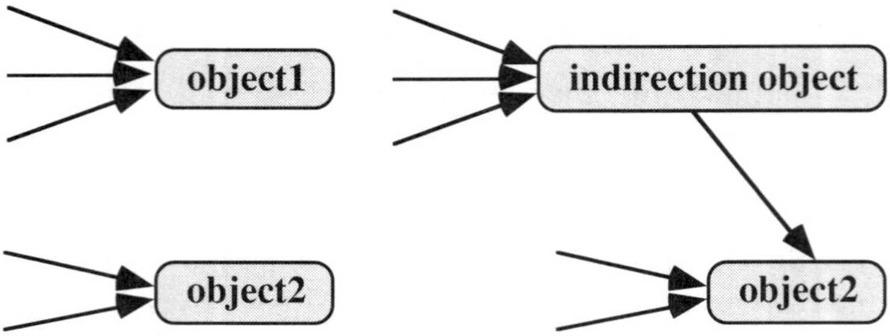

Figure 3.3 — Referencing objects through indirection objects.

that a new object is referenced, a check must be added to dereference it if necessary. The result is a global slowdown of the entire interpreter. A more efficient alternative is to make the indirection objects actual Smalltalk objects and have them indirect to their alternative receivers using **doesNot-Understand**:. This is the same approach that we took with disk objects. Clearly, inefficiency results but only for indirection objects. Moreover, indirection objects can be made to disappear over time by having the garbage collector function as described above. This approach was first described by Thomas, LaLonde, and Duimovich [2].

3.7 Extensions to the Disk Object Concept

With our design, it should be clear that a proper choice of external file and offset to be associated with a disk object must be made by some other mechanism. Even though disk objects transparently mutate into normal objects when first referenced, the converse does not hold. To facilitate offloading objects into files and converting them into disk objects, we need to extend class Object by adding instance operations like the following:

Listing 3.2 — Extensions to Class Object.

instance methods

offloading

offloadTo: fileName
    "Appends to the existing file."
    self **offloadTo**: fileName **executing**: []

```
offloadTo: fileName executing: aBlock
    "Appends to the existing file and executes the block before the object is mutated
    into a disk object. The block is expected to contain finalization code that must be
    executed before mutation is done."
    | file start end |
    file := File pathName: fileName.
    file position: (start := file size).
    "START OF STORE STRING VERSION
    string := self storeString.
    file putInteger: string size; nextPutAll: string.
    END OF STORE STRING VERSION"
    "START OF OBJECT FILER VERSION"
    ObjectFiler dump: self on: file.
    "END OF OBJECT FILER VERSION"
    file close.
    aBlock value.
    self become: (DiskObject new
        diskObjectFileName: fileName;
        diskObjectOffset: start)
```

Normally, it should be sufficient to use method **offloadTo:** to store objects into files and convert them to disk objects. Method **offloadTo:executing:** is provided for certain special objects that need finalization code before they are destroyed. For example, bitmaps must be released before they are mutated into disk objects. See the example methods in Listing 3.1 for sample uses.

3.8 Conclusions

We introduced the notion of disk objects to illustrate a number of powerful Smalltalk meta-operations and classes; e.g., the perform family of operations, **become:**, **doesNotUnderstand:**, and class Message. The **become:** operation, for example, can only be provided by programming environments that support garbage collection.

The notion of disk objects and the associated implementation details can be reused in several other applications:

- objects that support dynamic representations; i.e., that adjust to user accessing and modification patterns,

- non-intrusive monitoring of objects for measuring application dependent metrics,
- security applications that require special checks, permissions, and forwarding of requests,
- monitors for mutual exclusion in client/server applications, and
- remote objects that can be located over wide-area networks.

Each of these applications is based on the notion of encapsulating an interesting object by some other object that can intercept all the messages as illustrated in Figure 3.4.

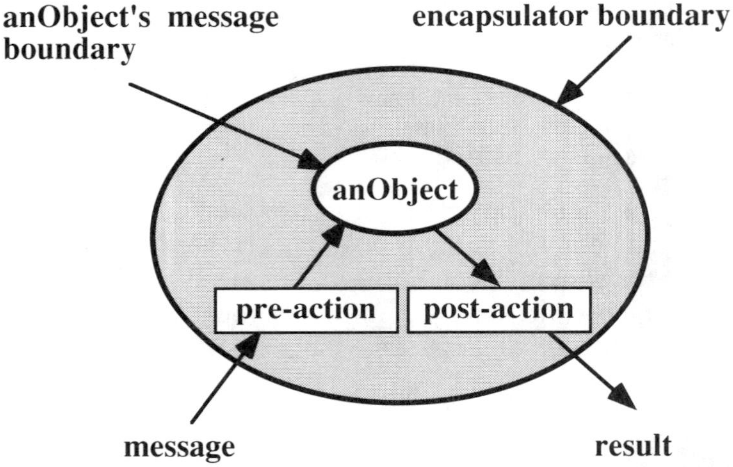

Figure 3.4 — Encapsulators in general.

3.9 References

1. Pascoe, G.A. Encapsulators: A New Software Paradigm in Smalltalk-80, Proc. OOPSLA '86, ACM SIGPLAN Notices, Vol. 21, No. 11, pp. 341-346, November 1986.

2. Thomas, D.A., LaLonde, W.R., and Duimovich, J., Efficient Support For Object Mutation and Transparent Forwarding, School of Computer Science Technical Report SCS-128, Carleton University, Ottawa, Canada, November 1987.

4

Film Loops and Primitive Animation

4.1 Introduction

To illustrate the use of Smalltalk bitmaps and simple display techniques, let's consider the design of a simple film loop facility. Film loops are never-ending movies and illustrate how simple animation sequences can be developed. The concept of disk objects introduced in Chapter 3 will be used to store sequences of still images. Techniques for obtaining flicker-free displays will also be introduced.

4.2 Film Loops: Never Ending Movies

A **film loop** is a never ending movie in which the end is spliced with the beginning; i.e., a circular sequence of frames repeatedly displayed at a fast enough rate to provide the illusion of smooth motion. Film loops are used in Videoworks II™ [1] for example, to provide rudimentary animated objects

---

1 VideoWorks II™, MacroMind Incorporated.

with a simple recurring behavior; e.g., a bird flapping its wings in flight or the flames in a fire. The speed at which the film loop is displayed is called the **frame rate**. For typical animation purposes, a frame rate of eighteen to twenty-four frames per second is normally used. Using the same sequence of still images with a faster frame rate results in speeded up motion; e.g., a fast flying bird.

The basic idea is to create a collection of frames as shown in Figure 4.1. Each frame is a bitmap. In the ideal situation, the bitmaps are constructed by a sophisticated animation system. More typically, they are hand-constructed with some kind of paint program. A base picture is first constructed. The second picture is constructed by slightly modifying a copy of the first. The third is a slightly modified version of the second and so on for as many still images as required. The pictures are then read into Smalltalk using some suitable utility. The details will vary from system to system. In our case, we constructed Paintbrush©[1] images and read them into Smalltalk using

aBitmap := Clipboard **getBitmap**.

On the other hand, bitmaps can also be created directly within Smalltalk, either by computing them (see **example1** in Listing 4.1) or by copying them from the screen (using "Bitmap **fromUser**").

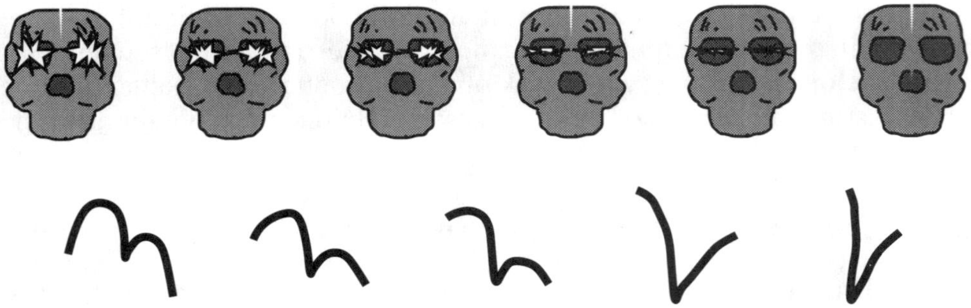

Figure 4.1 — A sequence of frames in a simple animation.

---

1 Microsoft Windows Paintbrush©, Microsoft Corporation.

4.3 Bitmaps in Brief

Generally, bitmaps are constructed by specifying an extent; i.e., the width and height as a point, by specifying an area of the screen from which the bits in bitmap are to come from, or by importing it from the clipboard as follows:

aBitmap := Bitmap **screenExtent**: aPoint
aBitmap := Bitmap **fromScreen**: aRectangle
aBitmap := Clipboard **getBitmap**

Subsequently, it is possible to inquire about the bitmap width, height, extent, and bounding box (a rectangle starting at 0@0 with the same extent as the bitmap). It is also possible to ask about the bitmap's pen (all bitmaps have pens associated with them) and to release the bitmap when we are done with it. Bitmaps must be released because the bits are kept in operating system memory. Such space is not automatically reclaimed by the garbage collector.

aBitmap **width**
aBitmap **height**
aBitmap **extent**
aBitmap **boundingBox**
aBitmap **pen**
aBitmap **release**

Bitmaps are copied onto other bitmaps (or colored) by asking their pens to do the copying (or coloring operation) using protocol such as the following:

destinationPen **copy**: sourcePen **from**: sourceRectangle **at**: destinationPoint
destinationPen **copy**: sourcePen ...as above... **at**: destinationPoint **rule**: aRopConstant
destinationPen **copy**: sourcePen **from**: sourceRectangle **to**: destinationRectangle
destinationPen **copy**: sourcePen **from**: ...as above... **rule**: aRopConstant
aPen **fill**: aColorConstant

The **from:at:** protocol ensures that the bitmap is copied without resizing. On the other hand, the **from:to:** protocol resizes the source rectangle bits to expand or contract into the area specified by the destination rectangle (the horizontal and vertical directions expand and/or contract independently). A **rule operation** (**rop** for short) such as **Srccopy** or **Srcand** indicates how the source and destination bits are to be merged. Although all of the boolean operations are permitted, it is difficult to predict their effects when color is involved. Additionally, there is no easy reference that can be used to obtain the complete list of rule constants. They are scattered randomly in WinConstants.

Method **example1** makes use of a Bitmap extension (**bitsAt**:**put**:, see below) that permits us to set the color of an individual bit in a bitmap.

```
bitsAt: aPoint put: aColor
    | oldColor |
    oldColor := self pen foreColor.
    self pen
        place: aPoint;
        foreColor: aColor;
        down;
        go: 1;
        up;
        foreColor: oldColor
```

4.4 A Film Loop Facility

Consider the **FilmLoop** class definition in Listing 4.1. Instances keep track of a name, the bitmaps in a collection called frames, another collection of associated offsets, and how long each frame is to be displayed. The latter is needed because the processor is generally too fast for small bitmaps albeit too slow for large ones. For small bitmaps, an extra delay is required to slow down the animation. Although the user provides the frame rate in frames per second, it is converted internally to the number of milliseconds per frame since the latter is more convenient for computing the required delay.

Every picture has a **hot spot**; i.e., a point that is considered to be the center of the picture for display purposes. For example, in the case of the birds, the hot spot would always be the middle of the body. When a series of animated pictures are displayed on a screen, the hot spot must remain fixed in spite of the fact that the individual pictures might be different sizes or that the wings might be flapping wildly above and below the body. The notion of a hot spot can be captured by associating an offset with the relevant bitmap. When the bitmap is displayed as part of an animation at a specified point, the offset (usually a negative amount) can be added to the original point to properly position the bitmap to keep the hot spot fixed.

Listing 4.1 — Class FilmLoop (exclusive of the display methods).

```
class name                FilmLoop
superclass                Object
instance variables        name frames offsets
                          millisecondsPerFrame
poolDictionaries          WinConstants ColorConstants

class methods

instance creation

new
    ^super new initialize

new: aFileName
    "Create a new film loop from disk information."
    ^self new name: aFileName

examples

example1
    "Create a film loop of increasing haze."
    "FilmLoop example1 followMouse release"

    | aLoop aCollection aBitmap location loopBitmap |
    aLoop := self new name: 'Haze'.
    aCollection := OrderedCollection new.
    aBitmap := Bitmap screenExtent: 60@60.

    aBitmap pen fill: ClrWhite.
    30 timesRepeat: [
        30 timesRepeat: [
            aBitmap
                bitsAt:
                    (Integer randomFrom: 0 to: 59) @
                    (Integer randomFrom: 0 to: 59)
                put: ClrRed].
        loopBitmap := Bitmap screenExtent: 60@60.
        loopBitmap pen
            copy: aBitmap pen from: aBitmap boundingBox at: 0@0.
        aCollection add: loopBitmap].

    aBitmap release.
    aCollection do: [:bitmap | aLoop add: bitmap].
```

aCollection **removeFirst**; **removeLast**; **reverseDo**: [:bitmap |
    loopBitmap := Bitmap **screenExtent**: 60@60.
    loopBitmap **pen**
        copy: bitmap **pen from**: bitmap **boundingBox at**: 0@0.
    aLoop **add**: loopBitmap].
^aLoop

examples

"FilmLoop1 := FilmLoop example1"
"FilmLoop1 unload"
"FilmLoop1 followMouse"
"FilmLoop1 displayFor: 10"
"FilmLoop1 release"
"Smalltalk removeKey: #FilmLoop1"
"(FilmLoop new: 'Haze') load; displayFor: 10; release"
"(FilmLoop new: 'Bird') load; followMouse; release"
"(FilmLoop new: 'Skull') load; followMouse; release"

instance methods

instance initialization

initialize

"Clear the film loop and set the default delay between frames."
frames := OrderedCollection **new**.
offsets := OrderedCollection **new**.
self **frameRate**: 24 "frames per second"

instance termination

release

frames **do**: [:aBitmap | aBitmap **release**]

accessing and modifying

frameRate

^(1000 "milliseconds per second" / millisecondsPerFrame) **rounded**

frameRate: framesPerSecond

millisecondsPerFrame := (1000 "milliseconds per second" / framesPerSecond)
    rounded.

name: aName

"Set the name of the film loop."
name := aName

loading and unloading

load

"Do nothing if already contains frames, else force the film loop into main memory (assume it is the first object in the file)."

```
frames isEmpty ifFalse: [^self].
^self become: (DiskObject new
    diskObjectFileName: name;
    diskObjectOffset: 0)
```

unload

"Save the film loop to disk."

```
self offloadTo: name executing: [self release]
```

adding bitmaps

add: aBitmap

"Add a bitmap to the film loop."

```
self add: aBitmap offset: (aBitmap extent // 2) negated
```

add: aBitmap **offset**: aPoint

"Add a bitmap to the film loop."

```
frames add: aBitmap.
offsets add: aPoint
```

delaying

delayToMatchFrameRate: millisecondsUsedSoFar

```
| delayAmount alarm |

delayAmount := (millisecondsPerFrame - millisecondsUsedSoFar) max: 0.
delayAmount > 0 ifTrue: [
    alarm := Time millisecondClockValue + delayAmount.
    [Time millisecondClockValue < alarm] whileTrue: []]
```

displaying

display: frame **at**: location **replacing**: background **at**: oldLocation

"Place the background back at oldLocation, copy the new background from location and place the frame on the screen. CODE SHOWN in Listing 4.2 and 4.3."

followMouse

"Follow the mouse until the button is pressed."

```
| repeat oldLocation oldBackground background startTime frameIndex
newLocation endTime |

"Handle the special case that almost never happens."
frames isEmpty ifTrue: [^self].
```

```
    "The usual situation."
    oldLocation := Cursor sense.
    background := Bitmap screenExtent: 0@0.
    startTime := Time millisecondClockValue.
    frameIndex := 0.
    Cursor hide.
    Notifier activeMainWindow captureMouseInput.
    Notifier consumeInputUntil: [:event |
        repeat := true.
        [repeat] whileTrue: [
            frameIndex := (frameIndex \\ frames size) + 1.
            newLocation := Cursor sense + (offsets at: frameIndex).
            oldBackground := background.
            background := self
                display: (frames at: frameIndex) at: newLocation
                replacing: background at: oldLocation.
            oldBackground release.
            oldLocation := newLocation.
            endTime := Time millisecondClockValue.
            self delayToMatchFrameRate: endTime - startTime.
            startTime := endTime.
            repeat := CurrentEvents isEmpty].
        event selector = #button1Down:].
    UserLibrary releaseCapture.

    Display pen
        copy: background pen from: background boundingBox at: oldLocation.
    background release.
    Cursor display

follow: positionBlock while: conditionBlock
    "While conditionBlock is true, animate the receiver at the position specified by
    positionBlock."

    | oldLocation oldBackground background startTime frameIndex newLocation
    endTime |

    "Handle the special case that almost never happens."
    frames isEmpty ifTrue: [[conditionBlock value] whileTrue: []. ^self].

    "The usual situation."
    oldLocation := positionBlock value.
    background := Bitmap screenExtent: 0@0.
    startTime := Time millisecondClockValue.
    frameIndex := 0.
```

```
    [conditionBlock value] whileTrue: [
        frameIndex := (frameIndex \\ frames size) + 1.
        newLocation := positionBlock value + (offsets at: frameIndex).
        oldBackground := background.
        background := self
            display: (frames at: frameIndex) at: newLocation
            replacing: background at: oldLocation.
        oldBackground release.
        oldLocation := newLocation.
        endTime := Time millisecondClockValue.
        self delayToMatchFrameRate: endTime - startTime.
        startTime := endTime].
    Display pen
        copy: background pen from: background boundingBox at: oldLocation.
    background release
displayFor: seconds
    "Show the film loop in the center of the screen for the given # of seconds."
    | startTime |
    startTime := Time millisecondClockValue.
    self
        follow: [Display boundingBox center]
        while: [(Time millisecondClockValue - startTime) / 1000 < seconds]
```

Method **examples** contains a number of comments with independent examples that can be executed. Method **example1** constructs a film loop of "haze" that randomly gets denser. It makes use of extensions to Integer for obtaining a random number and an extension to Bitmap for setting a specific bit in the bitmap (not shown). The method starts with a white bitmap and progressively darkens it by adding random red dots. Periodically, a copy is made and added to the film loop. To ensure that the film loop doesn't make an abrupt change when the switch from the last bitmap to the first occurs, a copy of the midsection of the original sequence (in reverse order) is appended to the film loop; i.e., a sequence of four still images would be stored as 1-2-3-4-3-2.

Following the samples in **examples**, the film loop of **example1** can be unloaded. Method **unload** files it out to disk in a file called 'Haze' in the current directory. This is done using method **offloadTo:executing:** implemented in class Object and described in Section 3.7. The 'Haze' film loop along with two others in corresponding files called 'Bird' and 'Skull' (assuming they are placed in the working directory) can be filed in using method **load**. This method assumes that a film loop with no frames (or bitmaps) resides on disk at offset 0. The film loop name is used as the file name to retrieve the disk version — a full path name like 'b:\filmloop.#4\bird' could be used instead of 'bird'. Method **load** achieves its intended goal by converting the film loop to a disk object. A subsequent message to the disk object (even one that simply prints or inspects it) will cause it to read the data from disk and mutate into the newly read object. The converse is achieved by method **load**. It simply offloads the film loop onto disk and releases all the bitmaps prior to mutating into a disk object. Subsequent use will mutate it back but a permanent copy will still reside on disk.

There is no need to actually use disk object representations of film loops. We can create film loops by simply adding bitmaps one at a time; e.g., by creating them in a paint program, importing them into Smalltalk using "Clipboard **getBitmap**", and adding them to the film loop using method **add**:. This method automatically constructs an offset that displaces the resulting picture by an amount that places its center at the display point. Any arbitrary offset can be specified using method **add**:**offset**: instead.

Methods **followMouse** (interactive) and **displayFor**: (non-interactive) are the two public methods illustrated in method **examples**. Method **displayFor**: makes use of **follow**:**while**: which is very similar to **followMouse**. At one time, we had hoped to create one general method that could be used for both purposes. Eventually, we gave up because there are some minor differences. It should be sufficient to consider just method **followMouse**. Since it is intended to animate the film loop at the cursor point, it must hide the cursor at the beginning and make it visible again at the end (using **hide** and **display**).

To have the film loop pictures follow the mouse, we must (1) capture all events until the user disconnects the mouse (by pushing the left button down), (2) dynamically display the film loop bitmaps at the cursor point, and finally (3) release the capture. Message **consumeInputUntil**: is actually a loop that cycles through each time an event occurs; e.g., when the mouse moves, when a mouse button is clicked, or when a character is typed. However, no activity will result in the loop if no events are generated (for example, when the mouse is held still). The notifier will actually go into a wait state until something occurs. To ensure that the film loop cycles continuously, we introduced an internal loop that exits only when external events get queued — this is checked via message "CurrentEvents **isEmpty**"; CurrentEvents is a global maintained by the system. In this way, we can guarantee that the notifier loop will immediately repeat rather than wait for the next external event (which would cause all activity on the screen to freeze).

The heart of the loop cycles through the frames one at a time. Variable frameIndex is used to keep track of the frame to be displayed. It starts at 1 (actually 0 but it is incremented the first time through), sequences through 2, 3, ..., all the way to "frame **size**" and then restarts at 1. Before a frame can be displayed, the picture beneath the previously displayed frame (the **background**) must be restored. Hence the need for a method that (1) displays the old background, (2) saves the part of the screen that will become the new background, and (3) displays the new frame. To avoid special case code, we start off with an old background that is an empty frame; i.e., a frame with extent 0@0. At the end, we also have to restore the very last background that was saved. This method, called **display**:**at**:**restoring**:**at**:, is discussed in detail in the next section.

4.5 Displaying Pictures: The Flicker Problem

Method "**display**: frame **at**: newLocation **restoring**: background **at**: oldLocation" is designed to work as illustrated in Figure 4.2. First, the background is restored, then the area to be wiped out by the new frame is picked up as the new background, and finally, the frame is displayed. By returning the new background, the process can be repeated with a new picture (or frame).

The detailed method is shown in Listing 4.2. It makes extensive use of the copying methods associated with bitmap pens. Note that the background is restored with rule Srccopy (use source bits only) whereas the new frame is displayed with rule Srcand (this ands the source and destination bits) to get a transparent effect.

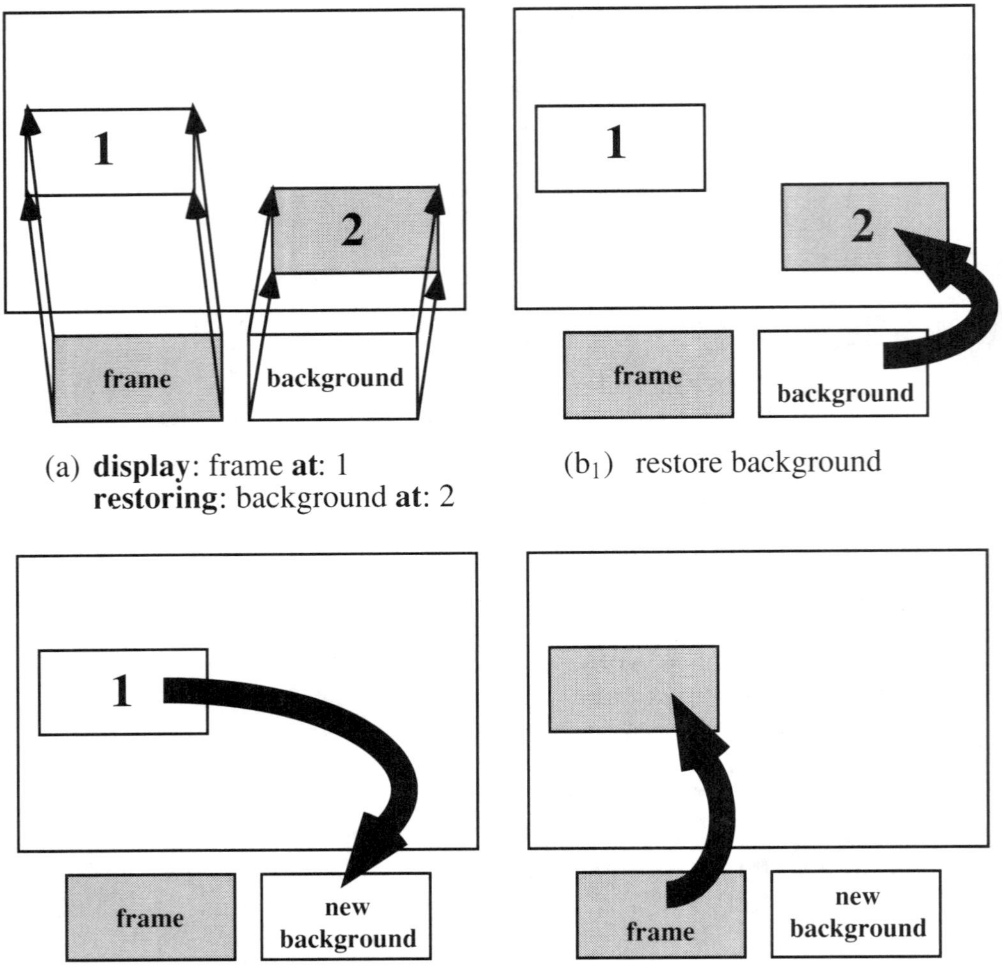

(a) **display**: frame **at**: 1
restoring: background **at**: 2

(b_1) restore background

(b_2) get new background

(b_3) display frame

Figure 4.2 — The three steps used by method **display:at:restoring:at:**.

Listing 4.2 — Instance method **display:at:restoring:at:** (with flicker).

```
displaying
display: frame at: location replacing: background at: oldLocation
    "Place the background back at oldLocation, copy the new background from
    location and place the frame on the screen."
    | newBackground newRectangle |
    "Restore the old."
    Display pen copy: background pen from: background boundingBox
        at: oldLocation rule: Srccopy.
    "Save area about to be overwritten for later restoring."
    newRectangle := location extent: frame extent.
    newBackground := Bitmap fromScreen: newRectangle.
    "Display the new."
    Display pen copy: frame pen from: frame boundingBox
        at: location rule: Srcand.
    ^newBackground
```

There is an important limitation to the display algorithm shown in Figure 4.2 — flicker is observed whenever the old background and the new frame intersect. Because the first display (to restore the screen to its original state) gets undone by the second, the eye easily discerns the discrete steps. This is not apparent without the overlap because the eye simply perceives them as being done in parallel.

The solution is to ensure that only one display step is used rather than two. This can be achieved by constructing the final image offscreen. More specifically, a copy of that part of the screen that contains both the frame and background areas is updated and this updated form is displayed in one step (see the revised **display:at:restoring:at:** method in Listing 4.3).

Listing 4.3 — Instance method **display:at:restoring:at:** (flicker free).

```
displaying

display: frame at: location replacing: background at: oldLocation
    "Place the background back at oldLocation, copy the new background from
    location and place the frame on the screen. To prevent flickering, only one copy
    operation to the screen is performed."

    | combinedRegion aBitmap newBackground |

    "Make a copy of that part of the screen that contains both the background area and
    the frame area."
    combinedRegion := (oldLocation extent: background extent)
        merge: (location extent: frame extent).
    aBitmap := Bitmap fromScreen: combinedRegion.

    "Restore the combined region to its original state."
    aBitmap pen copy: background pen from: background boundingBox
        at: oldLocation - combinedRegion origin rule: Srccopy.

    "Save the area to become the new background."
    newBackground := Bitmap screenExtent: frame extent.
    newBackground pen copy: aBitmap pen from: aBitmap boundingBox
        at: combinedRegion origin - location rule: Srccopy.

    "Display the new frame in the combined region."
    aBitmap pen copy: frame pen from: frame boundingBox
        at: location - combinedRegion origin rule: Srcand.

    "Finally, perform the one display operation to the screen."
    Display pen copy: aBitmap pen from: aBitmap boundingBox
        at: combinedRegion origin rule: Srccopy.
    aBitmap release.

    ^newBackground
```

4.6 Conclusions

This chapter served to introduce more of the bitmap facilities and allowed us to take advantage of disk objects introduced in Chapter 3. We also encountered the flickering problem and saw how it could be avoided by minimizing the number of display operations to the screen.

5

Windows, Panes, and Events

5.1 Introduction

The model-view-controller (MVC) framework in Smalltalk-80 is the same as the model-pane-dispatcher (MPD) framework in Smalltalk/V DOS (originally, V 286); i.e., view and pane are synonyms and so are controller and dispatcher. Nevertheless, the windowing classes in their respective libraries are entirely different. There are also major differences between different dialects of Smalltalk/V; e.g., V DOS and V Mac are MPD oriented while V for Windows and V for OS/2 use an entirely different philosophy. The latter two are fully event based and support a different framework which, for lack of a suitable name, we'll call the **event-driven** framework.

In this chapter, we will provide a brief description of the windowing system supported by Smalltalk/V for Windows (and Smalltalk/V for OS/2). To provide a reasonable case study, we will implement a simple English language translation facility. This will require an understanding of Smalltalk window events, a small part of the Windows (and OS/2) window library and philosophy, and the event-driven framework.

5.2 The Event-driven Framework

When creating a new application, a designer creates a subclass of ViewManager (see Figure 5.1). **View managers** (and consequently subclasses like YourApplication) are responsible for displaying the top-level title bar and other associated information like the system menu and zoom and collapse boxes, and also keep track of the panes they contain. Each application is responsible for interfacing with this top-level information and for inter-pane coordination; e.g., when an item is selected in a list pane, the application might respond by, for instance, changing the contents of a related text pane. This inter-pane coordination is achieved through Smalltalk window events; e.g., clicking on a button generates a #clicked event; clicking in a list pane generates a #select event. Since an application keeps track of its panes and is itself visible as a window when it is running, the terms application and application window are used interchangeably.

In addition to creating new application windows, designers may also need to create dialog windows for interactively querying the user of the application. A **prompter**, for example, is a window dialog. When creating a new dialog window, a designer creates a subclass of WindowDialog. **Window dialogs**, by contrast with normal applications, are modal — the originating window cannot continue until the modal window terminates and provides the information needed by the originating window.

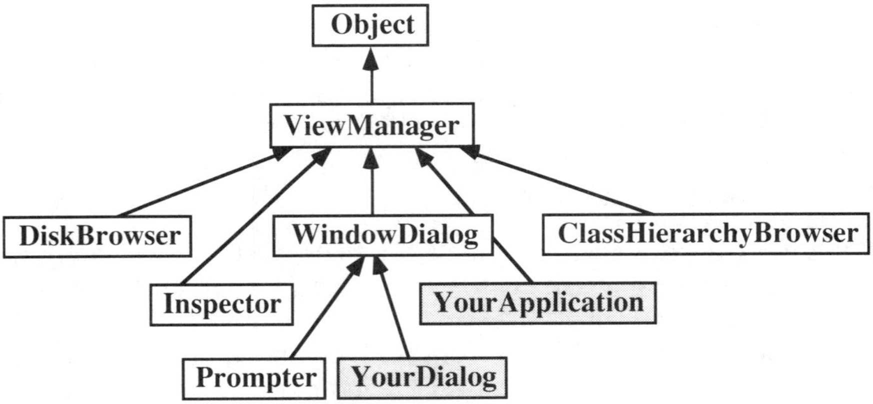

Figure 5.1 — Some view managers in Smalltalk/V.

A sampling of the class library that includes the major Pane classes is shown in Figure 5.2.

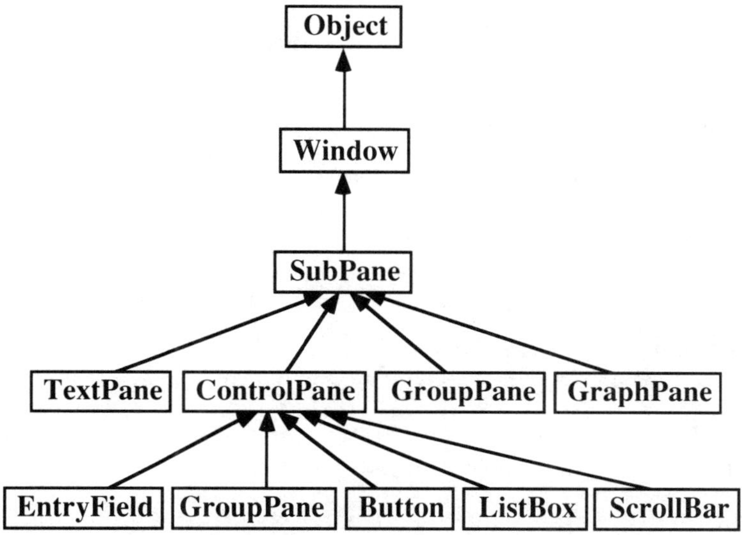

Figure 5.2 — Smalltalk/V partial window hierarchy.

5.3 Building an Application

To build an application, it is sufficient to create your own special subclass, create an **open** method that generates and adds subpanes to your application (window), and then executes **openWindow** as shown below:

```
open
    "Open a sample application."
    self labelWithoutPrefix: 'Sample Application'.
    self addSubpane: (PaneClass new
            event specification
            coloring specification
            layout specification
            pane specific specification
            yourself).
    self addSubpane: ...
        ...
    sefl addSubpane: ...
    self openWindow
```

The event related information is discussed in detail in the next section. The coloring information can be supplied by setting the foreground and background colors as follows:

```
aPane foreColor: colorConstant          (like ClrBlack)
aPane backColor: colorConstant          (like ClrGray)
```

Layout can be supplied as relative rectangles; e.g.,

```
aPane framingRatio: (Rectangle leftTop: 0@0 extent: (1/3)@(1/2)))
```

which indicates that the pane is to occupy 1/3 of the window in the horizontal direction and 1/2 of the window in the vertical direction. Alternatively, layout can be specified using framing blocks; e.g.,

```
aPane framingBlock: [:box | (
    Rectangle leftTop: box leftTop extent: box extent * (1/3)@(1/2)))
```

which computes the absolute size of the pane given the absolute rectangle for the entire window (supplied in parameter box).

Additionally, some panes need pane specific information; e.g., static text panes need to have specified whether or not the text is to be left justified, right justified, or centered.

Most of this information is easily specified using window builders — the subject of Chapter 6. The window builder itself generates the **open** method. It can be hand constructed but it is very cumbersome to do it manually particularly when ten or twenty panes are involved.

5.4 Smalltalk Window Events

Each pane has an **owner** which is normally the application. When a pane needs information specific to the application, it requests it indirectly from its owner via the Smalltalk event mechanism. A Smalltalk **window event** (not to be confused with events generated by the Windows (or OS/2) operating system) is generated by a pane either when it needs some information from the application or when it needs to tell the application that something significant has happened. Window events are not objects — they are represented by symbols; e.g., #clicked. To generate an event,

```
aPane event: #eventSymbol
```

is executed. In order for the application (or owner) to be able to respond to that event, the application must have provided the pane with a selector for an **event handler** (a standard Smalltalk method) as follows:

```
aPane when: #eventSymbol perform: #eventHandlerSelector:.
```

The event handler selector must have exactly one parameter which will be the pane in which the event was generated. Hence, the application must have a method such as the following:

```
eventHandlerSelector: aPane
    "Code to respond to event #eventSymbol."
```

The application then explicitly communicates with the pane to either get or change some attribute of the pane. It can also communicate with other panes by explicitly sending them messages or by generating events for them.

Panes can be named by executing:

```
aPane paneName: 'aName'
```

and once named, can be referenced by executing:

```
anApplication paneNamed: 'aName'.
```

Each kind of pane generates its own set of events. But there are a small set of common events that all panes generate. A summary of the most important ones, along with the expected application responses, is provided below:

Window Events

#opened

When generated: As a result of "opening" the application window just before the window appears on the screen.

Response: Perform initialization that can only be done after the panes are built; e.g., the title of the window, static information not supplied in the #getContents handler. You can't do this in method **initialize** because the panes don't exist at that time.

#close

When generated: As a result of attempting to "close" the application window.

Response: Perform finalization before the window disappears. Can confirm the close and either execute "self **close**" to really close or do nothing to cancel the close.

Common Events

#getPopUpMenu

When generated: User attempts to pop-up a menu.

Response: Set the pane's popup menu to an instance of Menu via message **setPopupMenu**:.

#getContents

When generated: A #getContents event is generated each time the message **update** is sent to the pane. Additionally, it is also generated (but once only) when the application is first opened. More specifically, when **open** is sent to the application, a #getContents event is generated for all panes, then an #opened event is generated, and finally the window appears on the screen.

Response: The pane is out-of-date. Do whatever is needed to make the pane be completely up-to-date; e.g., turn a radio button on if it should be on; provide a list pane with the list to be displayed and the item that should be selected; supply a text pane with the text to be displayed.

Text Pane Events

#save

When generated: When selecting save in the popup menu.

Response: Get the text from the text pane and process it in the application. Tell the text pane that it is no longer modified (using message **modified**:) so that it knows the text has been saved.

List Pane Events

#select

When generated: When the user clicks on an item in the list.

Response: Obtain the selection from the pane and respond to it.

#doubleClickSelect

When generated: When the user double clicks on an item in the list.

Response: Obtain the selection from the pane and respond to it.

Graph Pane Events

#button1Down
#button1DownShift
#button1Up
#button1DoubleClick
#button1Move (moving while button1 is down)
#button2Down
#button2Up
#button2DoubleClick
#button2Move (moving while button2 is down)
#mouseMove

When generated: As indicated.
Response: Respond to mouse movement or button clicking. The pane can be interrogated about the location of the mouse during the last event by sending it the message **mouseLocation**.

Button Pane Events

#clicked

When generated: When the user clicks on the button.
Response: Respond to clicking on the button.

In general, #getContents and #getPopupMenu are actually misnomers; they should be called #update (or #setContents) and #setPopupMenu respectively. Recall that a #getContents event is generated whenever a pane is out of date; e.g., when the window initially opens or when the pane is explicitly told to update itself (by sending it an **update** message). This is a fundamental notion that we will need to understand later.

A sample of the more interesting messages understood by panes is shown below.

Text Panes

aTextPane **contents**
Returns the string contained.
aTextPane **contents**: aString
Set it to the specified string.

aTextPane **modified**: aBoolean

After changes are made in a text pane, the modified instance variable becomes true. This method is useful for telling the application that the contents have been saved (by setting modified to false) in reaction to a #save event.

List Panes

aListPane **contents**

Returns the array (or ordered collection) of strings contained.

aListPane **contents**: aSequenceableCollection

Set it to the specified collection.

aListPane **selectedItem**

Returns the string selected (if one exists) or nil if nothing is selected.

aListPane **selection**: aStringOrNil

Set the item to be highlighted; nil means select nothing.

Buttons

aButton **contents**

Returns the string that is the label for the button.

aButton **contents**: aString

Sets the label.

aButton **selection**

Returns true if the button is on; false otherwise.

aButton **selection**: aBoolean

Sets the button on (true) or off (false).

Graph Panes

aGraphPane **mouseLocation**

Returns the current location of the mouse in *pane coordinates*.

For now, let's consider how the above notions can be put together to provide the event specification portion of an open method. Listing 5.1 provides a sample open method that associates a number of handlers with specific events and Listing 5.2 implements typical event handlers

Listing 5.1 — A sample **open** instance method.

```
open
    "Open a sample application."
    self labelWithoutPrefix: 'Sample Application'.
    self addSubpane: (TextPane new
        paneName: 'textPane';
        owner: self;
        when: #getContents perform: #textUpdate:;
        when: #save perform: #textSave:;
        when: #getPopupMenu perform: #textMenu:;
        framingRatio: (Rectangle leftTop: 0@0 extent: 2/3@1)).
    self addSubpane: (ListPane new
        paneName: 'listPane';
        owner: self;
        when: #getContents perform: #listUpdate:;
        when: #select perform: #listSelect:;
        when: #getPopupMenu perform: #listMenu:;
        framingRatio: (Rectangle leftTop: 2/3@0 extent: 1@(2/3))).
    self addSubpane: (Button new
        paneName: 'buttonPane';
        owner: self;
        contents: 'OK';
        when: #clicked perform: #buttonClicked:;
        framingRatio: (Rectangle leftTop: 1@(2/3) extent: 1@1)).
    self openWindow
```

An example of the sample application's responses to three of these events is shown in Listing 5.2. Except for **textMenu:**, most of the event handlers should be understandable on their own. In the **textMenu:** handler, labels are separated by a backslash character ('\') which are replaced by carriage returns using message **withCrs**. The '~' character causes the character following it to be underlined and usable as a keyboard speed key. The selectors are the names of methods to be executed when the corresponding menu item is selected. The selector message is sent to the owner of the menu (in this case, self, which is the application view manager).

Listing 5.2 — Sample event handlers.

the #getContents event handler for the text pane

```
textUpdate: aTextPane
    "Update the text pane by providing it with new text; e.g., the text contained by
    instance variable textPaneContents."
    aTextPane contents: textPaneContents
```

the #getPopupMenu event handler for the text pane

```
textMenu: aTextPane
    "Respond to popping up a text pane menu. Need to set the text pane's popup
    menu."
    | aMenu |
    aMenu := Menu
        labels: 'Item1 ~1\Item2 ~2\Item3 ~3' withCrs
        lines: #(2)
        selectors: #(itemOne itemTwo itemThree).
    aMenu
        title: 'Text Menu Title';
        owner: self.
    aTextPane setPopupMenu: aMenu

itemOne
    "Respond to clicking on the first item in the text menu."
    Transcript cr; show: 'Selected menu item 1'

itemTwo
    "Respond to clicking on the second item in the text menu."
    Transcript cr; show: 'Selected menu item 2'

itemThree
    "Respond to clicking on the third item in the text menu."
    Transcript cr; show: 'Selected menu item 3'
```

the #getContents event handler for the list pane

```
listUpdate: aListPane
    "Update the list pane by giving it a new list and a new selection"
    aListPane contents: #('Entry 1', 'Entry 2', 'Entry 3'); selection: 'Entry 2'
```

the #select event handler for the list pane

```
listSelect: aListPane
    "Respond to clicking on an entry in the list by recording the selected text in the
    textPaneContents instance variable and telling the text pane to update itself.
    NOTE: this will cause the text pane's #getContents handler to execute."
    textPaneContents := aListPane selectedItem.
    (self paneNamed: 'textPane') update
```

the #clicked event handler for the button

```
buttonClicked: aButtonPane
    "Respond to clicking on the OK button; e.g., by changing the contents of the
    textPaneContents instance variable and telling the text pane to update itself.
    NOTE: this will cause the text pane's #getContents handler to execute."
    textPaneContents := 'OK clicked on'.
    (self paneNamed: 'textPane') update
```

In general, there are two mechanisms for communicating with panes: explicitly telling it to update itself and implicitly via the **change/update** mechanism. The first technique is illustrated in method **itemOne** of Listing 5.2 by "(self **paneNamed**: 'textPane') **update**". It could alternatively be rewritten as "self **changed**: #textUpdate:" to use the change/update mechanism. The change/update mechanism itself is responsible for finding the pane with the specified #getContents handler. For a comparison between the two approaches see Figure 5.3.

Direct Messaging	Change/Update Mechanism
aPane **update**	self **changed**: #handler:
aPane **selector**	self **changed**: #handler: **with**: #selector
aPane **selector**: parameter	self **changed**: #handler: **with**: #selector **with**: parameter

• where *handler:* is the method name of the #getContents handler

Figure 5.3 — A comparison of direct messaging and the change/update mechanism.

The change/update mechanism was originally introduced to insulate the user from the implementation details of the panes. This held true when using the variation without selectors or parameters. However, most panes have a great deal of functionality that can be used to advantage in special applications. To access this functionality, explicit communication with the pane is needed. For example, a simple requirement for one pane to display tracing information while another pane executes can easily be handled by sending the tracing pane a "**nextPutAll**:" message. Trying to do this with "self **changed**: #handler:" all by itself is more difficult because the parameter cannot be passed directly. The only solution is store it in an instance variable that the handler can access directly. A better alternative is to say "self **changed**: #handler: **with**: #nextPutAll: **with**: text", but it seems contorted compared to "tracingPane **nextPutAll**: text".

Currently, Smalltalk/V uses a mixture of the two mechanisms — there are even situations like

```
aPane selection = 1
    ifTrue: [self changed: #handler with: #restoreSelected with: 1]
```

when the following would have worked just as well:

```
aPane selection = 1
    ifTrue: [aPane restoreSelected: 1]
```

On the other hand, the ability to name panes is a relatively recent addition to Smalltalk. Programming environment tools, like class hierarchy browsers, disk browsers, and debuggers, were implemented much earlier using the change/update mechanism and have not been modified.

It is up to the user to decide whether to use direct messaging or the change/update mechanism. Direct messaging requires the pane or the name of the pane whereas the change/update mechanism requires the name of the #getContents handler[1]. In the interest of simplicity and consistency, our current approach for Smalltalk/V for Windows and OS/2 is to use only direct messaging.

---

1 Another variation of the **changed**: message is available where the parameter is an arbitrary symbol. This variant (which is also used in programming environment tools) requires an implementation of method **update**: in the application where the parameter received is the symbol supplied.

5.5 A Sample Application

We illustrate the basic notions described in this chapter by implementing a simple language translation facility (see Figure 5.5). The window was actually designed with the window builder — a topic covered in the next chapter. But the event handlers required for the application were independently implemented. It is the event handlers that we will focus on here.

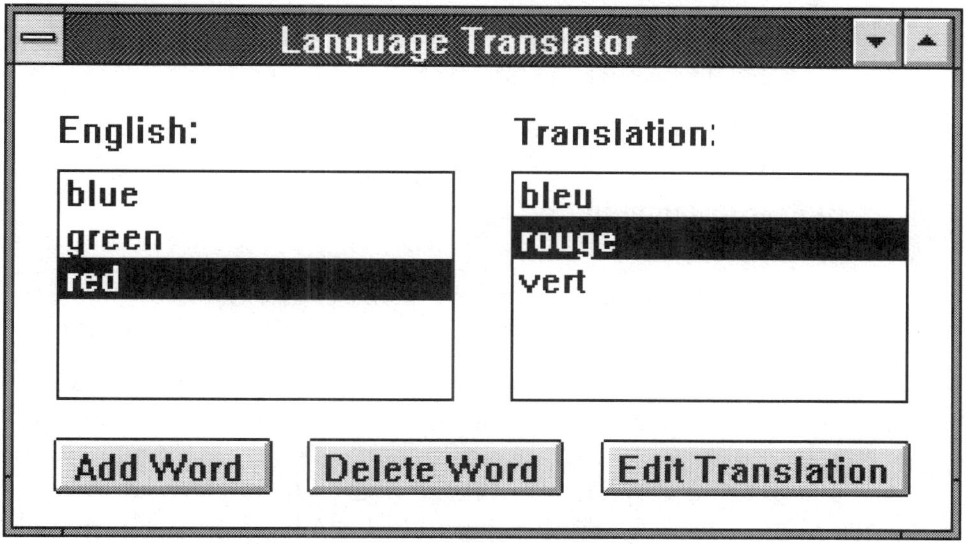

Figure 5.5 — The Language Translator application.

We make use of two list panes and three buttons. The leftmost list pane is the English pane while the other one is the translation pane. When we click on an entry in the English pane, the corresponding translation (in French) appears in the translation pane — and vice versa. Entries can be added to and removed from the English pane using the **Add Word** and **Delete Word** buttons respectively. The translation can be edited by clicking on the **Edit Translation** button.

We make use of the following event handlers (see Listing 5.3):

English pane
#getContents ⇒ updateEnglishList:
#select ⇒ selectEnglishItem:

Translation pane
#getContents ⇒ updateTranslationList:
#select ⇒ selectTranslationItem:

Add Word button pane
#clicked ⇒ clickedAddWord:

Delete Word button pane
#clicked ⇒ clickedDeleteWord:

Edit Translation button pane
#clicked ⇒ clickedEditTranslation:

LanguageTranslator view manager (TopPane)
#opened ⇒ opened: "Set up the initial list pane selection."

A good strategy to use for implementing an application is to ensure that the complete state of the application is maintained by a handful of instance variables. In our case, two variables are needed: **translation** which contains the mapping from English to French and **englishSelection** which specifies which English word is to be selected (nil is used if none are selected). From the English selection, we can infer the French selection. From this information, it is possible to completely update the application without considering any information maintained by the panes. When changes are made to the application (for example, by clicking in one of the panes), it is up to the handler to ensure that the state of the application is brought up-to-date.

Detailed comments are provided with each handler to help the reader understand the important aspects of the implementation.

Listing 5.3 — Class LanguageTranslator.

```
class                      LanguageTranslator
superclass                 ViewManager
instance variables         translation englishSelection

class methods

examples

example1
    "LanguageTranslator example1"
    self new openOn: (Dictionary new
        at: 'red' put: 'rouge';
        at: 'green' put: 'vert';
        at: 'blue' put: 'bleu';
        yourself)

WindowBuilder compatibility

wbCreated
    ^true

instance methods

opening

openOn: aDictionary
    "Sets the translation dictionary to aDictionary and then opens the application."
    translation := aDictionary.
    self open

open
    "WARNING!! This method was automatically generated by WindowBuilder.
    Code you add here which does not conform to the WindowBuilder API will
    probably be lost the next time you save your layout definition."
    | v |
    self addView: (
        v := self topPaneClass new
            owner: self;
            labelWithoutPrefix: 'Language Translator';
            noSmalltalkMenuBar;
            viewName: 'mainView';
            framingBlock: (FramingParameters new
                iDUE: 873@564; xC; yC;
                cRDU: (9@556 rightBottom: 864@46));
            pStyle: #(sysmenu sizable titlebar minimize maximize);
```

```
addSubpane: (
    StaticText new
        owner: self;
        framingBlock: (FramingParameters new
            iDUE: 158@32; lDU: 37 r: #left;
            rP: 5/22; tDU: 32 r: #top; bDU: 64 r: #top);
        startGroup;
        contents: 'English:';
        yourself);
addSubpane: (
    StaticText new
        owner: self;
        framingBlock: (FramingParameters new
            iDUE: 183@32; lP: 199/374; rP: 279/374;
            tDU: 32 r: #top; bDU: 64 r: #top);
        startGroup;
        contents: 'Translation:';
        yourself);
addSubpane: (
    ListPane new
        owner: self;
        framingBlock: (FramingParameters new
            iDUE: 366@294; lDU: 37 r: #left;
            rP: 8/17; tDU: 78 r: #top; bP: 62/85);
        paneName: 'englishPane';
        defaultStyle;
        startGroup;
        when: #getContents perform: #updateEnglishList:;
        when: #select perform: #selectEnglishItem:;
        yourself);
addSubpane: (
    ListPane new
        owner: self;
        framingBlock: (FramingParameters new
            iDUE: 366@294; lP: 9/17;
            rDU: 37 r: #right; tDU: 78 r: #top; bP: 62/85);
        paneName: 'translationPane';
        defaultStyle;
        startGroup;
        when: #getContents perform: #updateTranslationList:;
        when: #select perform: #selectTranslationItem:;
        yourself);
```

```
        addSubpane: (
            Button new
                owner: self;
                framingBlock: (FramingParameters new
                    iDUE: 199@62; lP: 8/187;
                    rP: 103/374; tP: 69/85; bP: 14/15);
                paneName: 'addWordButton';
                startGroup;
                when: #clicked perform: #clickedAddWord:;
                contents: 'Add Word';
                yourself);
        addSubpane: (
            Button new
                owner: self;
                framingBlock: (FramingParameters new
                    iDUE: 235@62; lP: 117/374;
                    rP: 10/17; tP: 69/85; bP: 14/15);
                paneName: 'deleteWordButton';
                startGroup;
                when: #clicked perform: #clickedDeleteWord:;
                contents: 'Delete Word';
                yourself);
        addSubpane: (
            Button new
                owner: self;
                framingBlock: (FramingParameters new
                    iDUE: 283@62; lP: 117/187;
                    rP: 179/187; tP: 69/85; bP: 14/15);
                paneName: 'editTranslationButton';
                startGroup;
                when: #clicked perform: #clickedEditTranslation:;
                contents: 'Edit Translation';
                yourself);
    yourself).
self openWindow
```

updating the entire application

update

```
"To update the entire application, it is sufficient to update both the English and Translation panes. Sending these panes update messages will cause #getContents events to be generated and the corresponding #getContents handlers updateEnglishList: and updateTranslationList: to execute."
(self paneNamed: 'englishPane') update.
(self paneNamed: 'translationPane') update
```

top pane #opened handler

```
opened: aPane
    "Handler for the #opened event in the top pane named 'mainView'. After all
    subpanes have been created, select the first item in the English pane (if any)."
    | englishPane |
    englishPane := self paneNamed: 'englishPane'.
    englishPane contents notEmpty ifTrue: [
        englishSelection := englishPane contents first.
        self update]
```

English pane #getContents handler

```
updateEnglishList: aPane
    "Handler for the #getContents event in the ListPane named 'englishPane'. Puts the
    most up to date list of English words into the English list pane and selects the most
    appropriate entry in the list."
    aPane
        contents: translation keys asSortedCollection;
        selection: englishSelection
```

English pane #select handler

```
selectEnglishItem: aPane
    "Handler for the #select event in the ListPane named 'englishPane'. When an entry
    in the english pane is selected, englishSelection is set to the selected English word.
    The translation pane is then told to update itself, which will cause the
    corresponding translation to be selected."
    englishSelection := aPane selectedItem.
    (self paneNamed: 'translationPane') update
```

translation pane #getContents handler

```
updateTranslationList: aPane
    "Handler for the #getContents event in the ListPane named 'translationPane'. Puts
    the most up to date list of translated words into the translation list pane and selects
    the most appropriate entry in the list."
    aPane
        contents: translation values asSortedCollection;
        selection: (translation at: englishSelection ifAbsent: [nil])
```

translation pane #select handler

```
selectTranslationItem: aPane
    "Handler for the #select event in the ListPane named 'translationPane'. When an
    entry in the translation pane is selected, englishSelection is set to the
    corresponding English word. The English pane is then told to update itself, which
    will cause the corresponding English word to be selected."
    englishSelection := translation
        keyAtValue: aPane selectedItem
        ifAbsent: [nil].
    (self paneNamed: 'englishPane') update
```

Add Word button pane #clicked handler

```
clickedAddWord: aPane
    "Handler for the #clicked event in the Button named 'addWordButton'. Prompts for
    the new word, and if a new word is supplied it is added to the translation
    dictionary and the list panes are updated accordingly."
    | response |
    response := Prompter prompt: 'New Word:' default: ''.
    response isNil | (response = '') "nil means cancelled"
        ifTrue: [^self].
    translation
        at: response
        put: (translation at: response ifAbsent: [response,' translation']).
    englishSelection := response.
    self update
```

Delete Word button pane #clicked handler

```
clickedDeleteWord: aPane
    "Handler for the #clicked event in the Button named 'deleteWordButton'. Asks the
    user to confirm deletion and if confirmed removes the selected item and its
    translation from the translator."
    englishSelection isNil
        ifTrue: [
            MessageBox message: 'You must select the English word to be deleted.']
        ifFalse: [(MessageBox
            confirm: 'Are you sure you want to delete ', englishSelection, '?')
                ifTrue: [
                    translation removeKey: englishSelection.
                    englishSelection := nil.
                    self update]
```

Edit Translation button pane #clicked handler

```
clickedEditTranslation: aPane
    "Handler for the #clicked event in the Button named 'editTranslationButton'.
    Verifies that a selection has been made, and if so, uses a dialog to ask the user to
    edit the existing translation."
    | newTranslation |
    englishSelection isNil
        ifTrue: [^MessageBox message: 'You must select the translation to be edited.'].

    (newTranslation :=
        Prompter
            prompt: 'Edit the translation:'
            default: (translation at: englishSelection)) isNil
        ifTrue: [^self]. "nil means cancelled"

    translation at: englishSelection put: newTranslation.
    (self paneNamed: 'translationPane') update
```

translation dictionary support

```
englishWordFor: aWord
    "Answer the English translation of aWord or nil if it is not found."
    ^translation
        keyAtValue: aWord
        ifAbsent: [nil]

translatedWordFor: anEnglishWord
    "Answer the translation of anEnglishWord or nil if not found."
    ^translation
        at: anEnglishWord
        ifAbsent: [nil]
```

5.6 Conclusions

In this chapter, we discussed what we referred to as the event-driven framework — a framework for building user interface driven applications in Smalltalk. We next reviewed the major windowing classes provided by Smalltalk/V for Windows and OS/2 and a small subset of the protocol most useful for implementing applications. Additionally, we provided considerable detail about Smalltalk window events and related these events to the windowing classes described above. Finally, we presented an application that illustrates how handlers can be written to implement a small but complete user interface driven application.

6

Taking the Pane out of Building Windows

6.1 Introduction

Smalltalk has long been regarded as one of the premier vehicles for building applications with sophisticated user interfaces. Now, window builders like Digitalk's PARTS™ (Parts Assembly and Reuse Tool Set), Objectshare Systems' Widgets/V 286 and WindowBuilder/V, the Tigre Programming Environment for ObjectWorks\Smalltalk from Tigre Systems, and VisualWorks from ParcPlace Systems promise to make it even easier. Let's see if that's the case. More specifically, let's consider building a small checking account management system similar to the popular Quicken product from Intuit Inc. using WindowBuilder/V.

6.2 The Checking Account Manager

The account manager is intended to permit an individual to keep track of transactions on several bank accounts. The user can create a new account, open an old account (which files it in), and save an account (which files it out). A list of transactions is kept for each account, sorted by date. Transactions are either deposits, withdrawals, or check payments. Moreover, each transaction can be decomposed into individual entries — an explanation plus a corresponding amount. Transactions may be created, modified, and deleted. Our objective is to demonstrate the use of Smalltalk and WindowBuilder/V as a vehicle for building a fairly sophisticated Windows application. To get a better feel for the goal, see Figure 6.1 which shows the user interface we designed and implemented.

Figure 6.1 — The account manager.

6.3 Using WindowBuilder/V

The window builder's main task is to provide an environment for interactively and visually choosing and laying out window components — a MacDraw or CorelDraw for windows, so to speak. Once the design of the user interface is complete, it is simply a matter of **saving** the window — this implies the construction or modification of a new window class and the production of code to generate the user interface.

Once the WindowBuilder package has been installed, it is invoked via a simple menu that has been added to the Transcript window. It opens as shown in Figure 6.2.

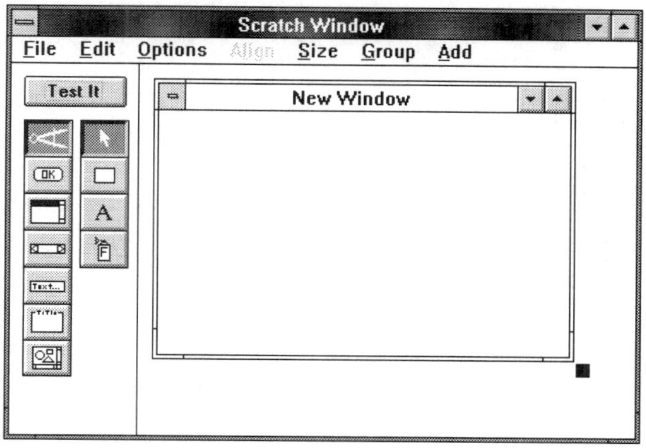

Figure 6.2 — WindowBuilder/V on a new window.

There are two columns of icons on the left side of the builder. The leftmost allows the user to select a category of standard user interface parts; e.g., buttons, list panes, scroll bars, text panes, group boxes, and graph panes. Once a category has been selected, the right column displays the choices available within that category. For example, in Figure 6.3, the button category (dark OK in the left column) is selected. The right column shows the 5 different button styles available — in this case, called respectively — the (generic) button, drawn button, check box, three-state button, and radio button. Clicking on the three-state button tool (2nd from the bottom in the right column), for example, causes the cursor to change into a cross hair. This implies that the user should click-drag to create a new three-state button in the **layout area** — the central right area of the builder. When the mouse button is released, a new three-state button is drawn. It can be resized and repositioned at will. Figure 6.3 actually shows the result after three check boxes, two generic buttons, and one group box have been added.

The bottom area provides access to the parameters for the actual part selected in the layout area. In the case of Figure 6.3, the entire window (the top pane) is selected rather than an internal part. Hence the window title can be edited — we titled this simple window "Color Picker". Clicking on **Menu** allows the menu bar to be specified (not shown).

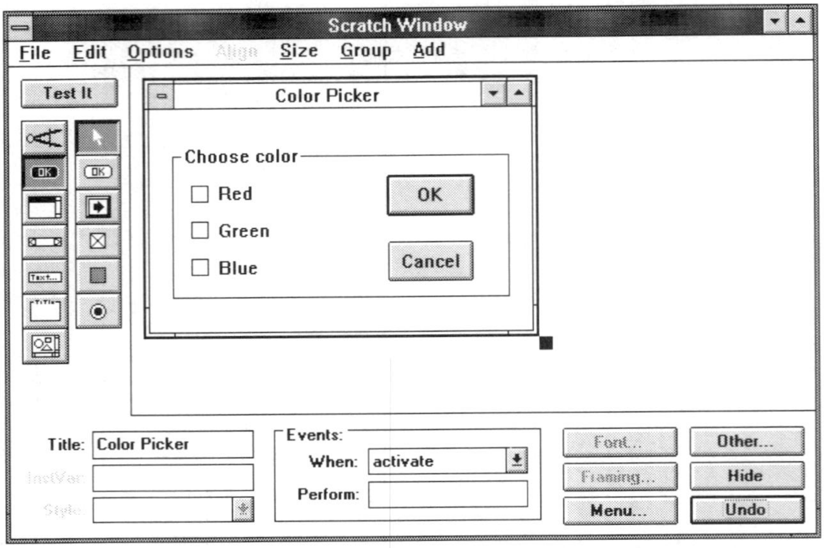

Figure 6.3 — Creating a simple user interface with the WindowBuilder.

In the case of the checking account manager, we had a reasonably close approximation of our intended interface after a few hours. However, we made many changes over the next few days before it appeared as shown in Figure 6.1. For example, many components had to be lined up and adjusted to have identical width and/or height — a requirement that was easy to do via the **Align** and **Size** menu items. Interface windows that are too large to fit entirely within the layout area can also be scrolled.

In Figure 6.4, the **Deposit** radio button is selected. At the bottom of the builder, we have specified several attributes; e.g., (1) the title appearing in the button is **Deposit**, (2) when the radio button is clicked, the message "**setType**: radiobutton" will be sent to our application window — the parameter allows us to determine which of the three buttons was clicked by interrogating the contents of the pane, the title in this case. Not shown is the fact that we can change the font of the title, specify the new position and size of the button when the window is resized, and provide pop-up menus for text panes (in our case, we haven't used any).

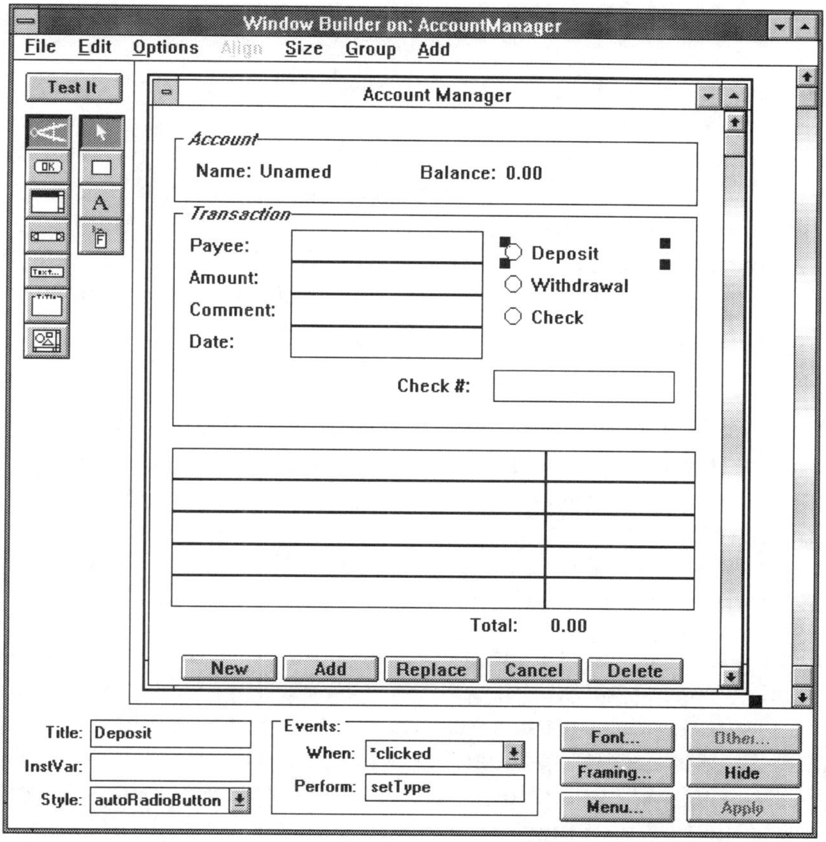

Figure 6.4 — The account manager user interface under construction.

One of the necessary features of a builder is the capability to save the new interface in a class. Additionally, it must be possible to start writing the methods to support the application and then make changes by simply invoking the builder on the existing class. We had to go back and forth dozens of times. As everyone expects, positioning and laying out the user interface components with an interface builder is clearly much superior to the hand-written coding approach.

6.4 Generating An Account Manager Prototype

There is more to writing an application than providing a "mock up" of the user interface. As generated by the builder, the interface is sterile. You can click on the buttons and type in the entry fields but you will elicit no response. So what does the builder actually generate? First, it generates a class for the application window — it prompted us for the name; we called it **AccountManager**. Second, it generates enough methods to provide a starting point for future additions. As a minimum, it generates methods

wbCreated
open

The first is a small class method returning true. The second is an instance method that constructs and initializes all the panes before opening a window containing these panes. In our case, it is quite large. This **open** method is not normally hand-modified because it is regenerated by the builder whenever the interface is re-edited and saved. See Listing 6.1 for the class definition and portions of the above methods.

The builder will also generate event handler methods if they do not already exist. For example, in Figure 6.4, we specified **setType**: as the handler for the Deposit radio button's **#clicked** event. Since method **setType**: does not already exist in our application, it is automatically generated by the builder — as a method containing only a comment. It is up to us to make additions to this method to actually make it do something useful.

The account manager needs to keep track of the current account, the transaction being worked on, and the name of the file into which the account is to be subsequently saved. An account maintains a sorted collection of transactions (currently sorted by date although we could have sorted it differently) while a transaction provides information such as the payee, the total amount of the transaction, and the transaction type (a symbol such as #Check or #Deposit). Since these classes are relatively simple and secondary to this application, we will assume they exist. To be able to cancel a transaction, it is necessary to keep the old transaction (including an index into the list of transactions for convenience) and work on a copy — hence the need for an instance variables like workingTransaction. The result is a class definition like the following:

Listing 6.1 — The AccountManager class.

class	AccountManager
superclass	ViewManager
instance variables	account transactionIndex transaction workingTransaction fileName validationSelectors entryNamePanes entryAmountPanes
pool dictionaries	ColorConstants WBConstants WinConstants

```
class methods
examples

examples
    "AccountManager new open"
    "AccountManager new openOn: Account new"

instance methods
instance initialization

initialize
    super initialize.
    account := Account new.
    self cacheTransactionAt: 0.
    fileName := ''.

cacheTransactionAt: index
    transactionIndex := index.
    transaction := transactionIndex = 0
        ifTrue: [Transaction new]
        ifFalse: [account at: transactionIndex].
    workingTransaction := transaction copy.

opening

openOn: anAccount
    "Open on an existing account."
    account := anAccount.
    self cacheTransactionAt: account size; open.
```

Listing 2 contains the two major builder generated methods. Only a small portion of **open** method is shown — that part which generates the code to construct the **Deposit** button of Figure 6.4. Notice that the name of the button is stored in the radio button along with two event handlers (more on this later), its contents — the string 'Deposit', and a framing block (machine readable but not human readable) that can recompute the new size and position should the window be reframed. In total, close to 40 subpanes were needed to construct the account manager interface. At the end of method **open** is the code to generate the **File** menu shown in Figure 6.5. For each menu item, we had to provide a label, an accelerator key, and the name of the method to be invoked when the menu item is selected.

Listing 6.2 — The methods generated by the builder.

```
class methods
window builder additions
wbCreated
    ^true

instance methods
window builder additions
open
    "WARNING This method was automatically generated by WindowBuilder. Code
    you add here which does not conform to the WindowBuilder API will probably be
    lost the next time you save your layout definition."
    | v |
    self addView: (
        v := self topPaneClass new
            owner: self;
            labelWithoutPrefix: 'Account Manager';
            noSmalltalkMenuBar;
            viewName: 'mainView';
            framingBlock: (FramingParameters new
                iDUE: 1029 @ 968; xC; yC;
                cRDU: (14 @ 956 rightBottom: 1015 @ 88));
            pStyle: #(sysmenu maximize minimize sizable titlebar);
            when: #close perform: #close:;
            when: #opened perform: #opened:;
```

```
            addSubpane: (
                RadioButton new
                    owner: self;
                    framingBlock: (FramingParameters new
                        iDUE: 274 @ 32; lDU: 603 r: #left; rDU: 878 r: #left;
                        tDU: 200 r: #top; bDU: 232 r: #top);
                    startGroup;
                    tabStop;
                    when: #getContents perform: #getType:;
                    when: #clicked perform: #setType:;
                    contents: 'Deposit';
                    yourself);
            "... close to 39 more panes ..."
        yourself).
    v menuWindow
        yourself;
        addMenu: (
            Menu new
                title: 'File';
                owner: self;
                appendItem: 'New Alt+N' selector: #newAccount
                    acceleratorString: 'Alt+N';
                appendItem: 'Open Alt+O' selector: #openAccount
                    acceleratorString: 'Alt+O';
                appendSeparator;
                appendItem: 'Save Alt+S' selector: #saveAccount
                    acceleratorString: 'Alt+S';
                appendItem: 'Save As Alt+A' selector: #saveAccountAs
                    acceleratorString: 'Alt+A').
self openWindow
```

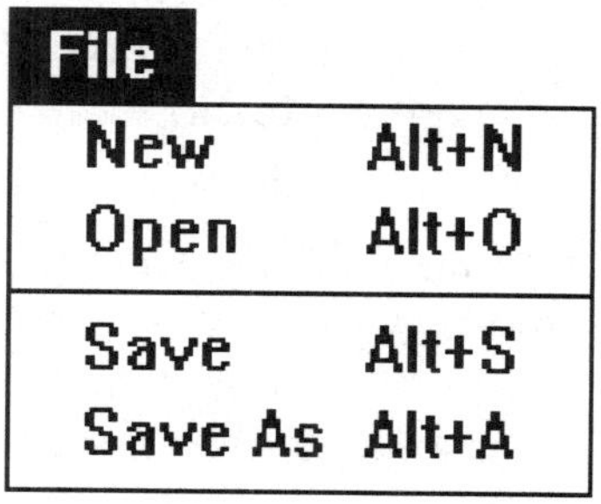

Figure 6.5 — The account manager's menu bar (the File menu).

As generated, the interface can be used by invoking "AccountManager **new open**" — the builder has a **Test It** button that does precisely this. Presumably, all of the standard windowing facilities that we expect of windows is provided by the panes and the view manager (our account manager) itself. The following sequence of steps is involved in starting up the interface:

1. What **new** does:
    - Create a new window.
    - Execute **initialize**.
2. What **open** does:
    - Create the subpanes, add them to the window, and build a menu bar.
    - Execute **initWindow** (if one is supplied by the application).
    - Ask each pane to update itself by generating a #getContents event for each of them — if a handler was specified, this handler will execute.
    - Generate an #opened event. If a handler was specified, this handler will execute.
    - Display the window on the screen.
    - Give the window control.

Inherited method **initialize** performs the initialization required by the window (the view manager) at creation time. To add initialization code specific to our application, we can simply override the methods while making sure that the original method via "super ..." is still executed. Method **initWindow** is executed only if one is provided. An equivalent sequence is executed when the user attempts to close the window via the close box:

3. What an attempt to close the window's close box does:
    - Generate an #close event. If a handler was specified, this handler will execute. It can specifically close the application by sending itself the **close** message or do nothing and cancel the close.
    - Destroy and remove the window if an explicit **close** message was sent or if no #close handler was provided.

In our case, the **opened**: event handler assumes workingTransaction has already been set up and initializes a number of the instance variables as identity dictionaries: validationSelectors, entryNamePanes, and entryAmountPanes. These variables are intended to be used as follows:

validationSelectors **at**: aPane ⇒ selector (the name of a validation method)
entryNamePanes **at**: aPane ⇒ index of the pane (an integer from 1 to 5)
entryAmountPanes **at**: aPane ⇒ index of the pane (an integer from 1 to 5)

The full text of the method consists of the following:

opened/close event handlers

```
opened: aPane
    "Set up the instance variables, and the window."

    | payeePane amountPane commentPane datePane checkNumberPane
    entryNamePane1 entryAmountPane1 entryNamePane2 entryAmountPane2
    entryNamePane3 entryAmountPane3 entryNamePane4 entryAmountPane4
    entryNamePane5 entryAmountPane5 sliderPane accountNamePane
    accountBalancePane totalPane |

    "Get local names for the panes."
    payeePane := self paneNamed: 'payeePane'.
    amountPane := self paneNamed: 'amountPane'.
    commentPane := self paneNamed: 'commentPane'.
    datePane := self paneNamed: 'datePane'.
    checkNumberPane := self paneNamed: 'checkNumberPane'.
    entryNamePane1 := self paneNamed: 'entryNamePane1'.
    entryAmountPane1 := self paneNamed: 'entryAmountPane1'.
    entryNamePane2 := self paneNamed: 'entryNamePane2'.
    entryAmountPane2 := self paneNamed: 'entryAmountPane2'.
    entryNamePane3 := self paneNamed: 'entryNamePane3'.
    entryAmountPane3 := self paneNamed: 'entryAmountPane3'.
    entryNamePane4 := self paneNamed: 'entryNamePane4'.
    entryAmountPane4 := self paneNamed: 'entryAmountPane4'.
    entryNamePane5 := self paneNamed: 'entryNamePane5'.
    entryAmountPane5 := self paneNamed: 'entryAmountPane5'.
    sliderPane := self paneNamed: 'sliderPane'.
    accountNamePane := self paneNamed: 'accountNamePane'.
    accountBalancePane := self paneNamed: 'accountBalancePane'.
    totalPane := self paneNamed: 'totalPane'.

    "Initialize the contents of most panes and create dictionaries
    that group some of them together."
```

```
datePane contents: workingTransaction date printString.
accountBalancePane contents: (self stringFromCents: account balance).

entryNamePanes := IdentityDictionary new
    at: entryNamePane1 put: 1; at: entryNamePane2 put: 2;
    at: entryNamePane3 put: 3; at: entryNamePane4 put: 4;
    at: entryNamePane5 put: 5; yourself.
entryAmountPanes := IdentityDictionary new
    at: entryAmountPane1 put: 1; at: entryAmountPane2 put: 2;
    at: entryAmountPane3 put: 3; at: entryAmountPane4 put: 4;
    at: entryAmountPane5 put: 5; yourself.

validationSelectors := IdentityDictionary new
    at: checkNumberPane put: #validateCheckNumber:;
    at: payeePane put: #validatePayee:;
    at: amountPane put: #validateAmount:;
    at: commentPane put: #validateComment:;
    at: datePane put: #validateDate:;
    yourself.

entryNamePanes keys do: [:field |
    validationSelectors at: field put: #validateEntryName:].
entryAmountPanes keys do: [:field |
    validationSelectors at: field put: #validateEntryAmount:].

close: aPane
    self canDiscardAccount ifFalse: [^self].
    self close
```

6.5 Bringing the Account Manager to Life

In order to make the application respond to user interface interactions, we need to

- provide methods for menu bar processing — **newAccount**, **openAccount**, **saveAccount**, and **saveAccountAs**.
- specify how each pane (button, entry field, etc) should initialize itself from information in the application — the **#getContents** event handlers.
- specify how special panes should respond to user initiated activity; e.g., (1) the **#clicked** event handler for buttons, (2) the scrolling event handler for the scroll bar.

- provide a mechanism to be able to tab from one entry field to the next and for the information in numeric fields to be automatically validated and entered; e.g., to update the total at the bottom.
- provide a mechanism in the handlers to be able to process inter-pane interactions; e.g., when the **Check** radio button is pressed, the **Deposit** button (see Figure 6.1) should be turned off; when a new transaction is added, the account **balance** should be updated.

6.6 *Radio Button Handling*

Let's begin by giving life to the deposit, withdrawal, and check buttons shown in Figure 6.6. In the builder, we specified the corresponding **#getContents** and **#clicked** event handlers. Rather than specify 2 each for a total of 6, we provided 2 generic ones.

Figure 6.6 — The transaction type radio buttons.

We called the #getContents event handler **getType**: (to update the user interface by getting the type from the application) and the #clicked event handler **setType**: (to reset the application's type from the data in the radio button that was clicked). In retrospect, it might have been better if we had renamed these handlers **updateRadioButton**: (for **getType**:) and **clickedRadioButton**: (for **setType**:). Perhaps we'll adopt such a strategy for future applications.

radio button #getContents handler

getType: aPane
"Get the new transaction type (#Check, #Widthdrawal, or #Deposit) and turn the button on if it matches the working transaction type; off otherwise."
aPane **selection**: (workingTransaction **type asString** = aPane **contents**)

radio button #clicked handler

```
setType: aPane
    "Set the working transaction type from the radio button' label (or contents)."
    workingTransaction type: aPane contents asSymbol
```

In general, the pane supplied as parameter is the pane in which the event occurred; i.e., the specific pane being queried or clicked. Clearly, we have to know how buttons work to write this code; e.g., we have to know that **contents** retrieves the button label such as 'Deposit' and that **selection**: turns the button on or off with a boolean.

When a radio button is out of date and told to update (either as a consequence of the window opening or because we explicitly sent an **update** message to the button), a #getContents event is generated. It is then the task of our handler, **getType**, to get the type information from the application and update the user interface by either turning the button on or off. In our case, we want it to be on if the working transaction's type (one of #Check, #Widthdrawal, or #Deposit) matches the contents of the button and off otherwise.

When a user clicks on one of the radio buttons, it is the task of the #clicked handler, **setType**:, to set (record) the type information in some suitable place in the application; e.g., in the working transaction. So we simply obtain the information from the button (its content) and record it.

When a particular radio button is clicked on, nothing special was done in the code to cause the other radio button (the one that used to be on) to suddently turn off. The builder permits radio buttons to be grouped together so that only one is ever on at a time.

6.7 Entry Pane Processing and Validation

Next, consider giving some functionality to the 5 transaction entry amount panes — currently with amounts 200.00 and 75.00 in Figure 1. In particular, after typing a new amount and hitting return or tabbing to the next entry field, the amount should be validated and a new total displayed.

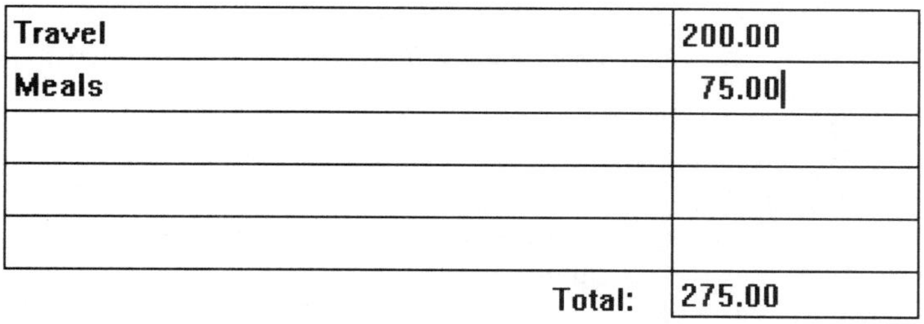

Figure 6.7 — The transaction entry name, entry amount, and total panes.

In general, different entry fields must be validated and recorded in different ways. For example, the comment field can be trivially accepted and recorded, the date field must be validated with a fairly lengthy though straightforward algorithm, while an entry amount must be checked to see if it is a valid dollar amount. To handle each situation, it is convenient to set up a dictionary of validation selectors — one per entry field. We did this in the #opened event handler that maps each entry field pane to the corresponding selector. A **perform:with:** can then be used to execute the correct method.

Key	***Value***
datePane	#validateDate:
...	...
entryAmountPane1	#validateEntryAmount:
...	...
entryAmountPane5	#validateEntryAmount:
...	...

At some point, validation for a specific pane can be done by executing a generic method like the following:

```
validatePane: aPane
    | selector |
    selector := validationSelectors at: aPane ifAbsent: [^self].
    ^self perform: selector with: aPane.
```

A specific validation method like **validateEntryAmount**: could be designed to validate and record the new amount, in addition to computing and displaying the new total. If validation fails, a complaint can be issued (we'll come back to that later) and the validation activity terminated.

```
validateEntryAmount: aPane
    "Validate and record amount. Return if        successful."
    | amount entryIndex |
    amount := self centsFromString: aPane contents
        ifFail: [self complain. ^false].
    entryIndex := entryAmountPanes at: aPane.
    workingTransaction entryAmountAt: entryIndex put: amount.
⇒   (self paneNamed: 'totalPane') update.
    ^true
```

To ensure that the total pane updates itself properly, a **#getContents** handler (say called **updateTotal:**) must be supplied that is sufficiently clever to compute the new total.

```
updateTotal: aPane
    "The #getContents handler for the total pane)."
    aPane contents: (self stringFromCents: self totalOfEntryAmounts)

totalOfEntryAmounts
    "Sum up the category amounts. Uninitialized entries are 0."
    | sum |
    sum := 0.
    1 to: workingTransaction size do: [:index |
        sum := sum + (workingTransaction entryAmountAt: index)].
    ^sum
```

As a rule, there are at least two ways of providing feedback about entries that fail the validation test:

- **intrusive feedback** that forces the user to acknowledge (and perhaps even to fix) the incorrect entry; e.g., via MessageBoxes.
- **unobtrusive feedback** that lets the user know about the problem without forcing him to do anything specific about it; e.g., by changing the color of an invalid pane.

The latter is clearly superior for high volume work. A good typist can come back later to fix the error rather than fix it as it occurs. To handle such an approach, a few small changes are needed to method **validatePane:**.

```
validatePane: aPane
    "Validate aPane and provide visual feedback if it fails. Return whether or not
    successful."
    | selector result |
    "Determine if its the kind of pane that needs validation."
    selector := validationSelectors at: aPane ifAbsent: [^true].
    result := self perform: selector with: aPane.
    self provideFeedbackFor: aPane validated: result.
    ^result

provideFeedbackFor: aPane validated: aBoolean
    "Make invalidated panes be red; others are the mainview color."
    aBoolean
        ifTrue: [aPane backColor: self mainView backColor]
        ifFalse: [aPane backColor: ClrRed].
    aPane invalidateRect: nil. "needed to force the new color to be visible"
```

If validation fails, we color the pane red. If it succeeds, the pane is colored the same as the main view's background color (it might have been previously red). Method **invalidateRect:** forces the system to redraw the pane. A rectangle can be supplied to indicate which part of the pane is invalid; if nil is provided, the entire pane is assumed to be invalid. To make this work in the presence of user supplied pane colors, we would have to save the old colors — a relatively simple extension. Additionally, the validation routines must no longer explicitly complain; e.g., method **validateEntryAmount:** must simply return false when validation fails.

The same strategy can also be used to provide feedback with respect to the total field. This particular field must be the sum of the entry amount panes. But it must also match the value provided in the transaction **Amount** field (see Figure 6.1). Unobtrusive feedback can be provided by writing the total pane's #getContents handler, method **updateTotal:**, as follows:

```
updateTotal: aPane
    "The #getContents handler for the total pane."
    "Sum up the total for the category amount column and validate
     the total against the working transaction amount."
    | total |
    total := self totalOfEntryAmounts.
    aPane contents: (self stringFromCents: total).
    self
        provideFeedbackFor: aPane
        validated: total = workingTransaction amount abs
```

One final important point about the validation methods is that they must be executed for all associated entry fields whenever a transaction is to be recorded with **Add** or **Replace**, for example. In general, it is possible to switch from one entry field to another by clicking with the mouse without typing cr or tab. Some entries could be skipped entirely. So validation does not always occur at the time new entries are typed in.

One last issue involves tabbing. As a rule, tabbing advances "focus" to the "next" registered field. We can specify the tabbing order (and which fields are to be skipped) using the builder. Additionally, we can specify what is to happen when a user hits tab or carriage return after typing or advancing focus to an entry field. Two events, **#gettingFocus** and **#losingFocus**, are useful for that purpose. In our case, it is sufficient to associate the handler **validatePane**: with the #losingFocus event.

6.8 Scrolling Through Transactions

Scroll bars requires more event handlers than any other pane. In particular, they need handlers for

- **#nextLine** (move down 1 unit)
- **#nextPage** (move down many units)
- **#prevLine** (move up 1 unit)
- **#prevPage** (move up many units)
- **#sliderPosition** (move to specific unit)
- **#home** (move to top)
- **#end** (move to bottom)

in addition to **#getContents**. The **position** of a scroll bar is defined to be an integer between specifiable **minimum** and **maximum** values. Scrolling with the arrow heads moves by an integer amount called the **line increment**; clicking in the scroll area causes faster scrolling; i.e., by an amount called the **page increment**. Hitting the “home” and “end” keys causes the scroll bar to instantly move to the top or bottom respectively.

In general, the slider must be re-initialized whenever a new account is opened or a transaction is added or removed (since the maximum has to change). In our case, we decided to have s**low** scrolling jump 1 transaction at a time and f**ast** scrolling jump by a fifth (20%) of the transactions in the account. This can be handled with a **#getContents** handler such as the following:

```
updateSlider: aPane
  | limit |
  aPane
    minimum: 1;
    maximum: (limit := account size max: 1);
    lineIncrement: 1;
    pageIncrement: (account size // 5 max: 1);
    position: (transactionIndex = 0
        ifTrue: [limit]
        ifFalse: [transactionIndex])
```

Moving the slider implies moving to a new transaction. There are two possible cases:

- the current transaction is valid and has been accepted ⇒ **move** and update.
- the current transaction is invalid (e.g., totals do not agree) or was not accepted when the user was prompted ⇒ **do NOT move** (and reposition the slider to where it used to be).

Clearly, we need to keep track of the working transaction and its position in the account so that we can **potentially back up** to it. We can get away with the same handler for each of the slider events if we ask the slider pane for the new position that it moved to. The handler would then appear as follows:

```
sliderPosition: aPane
    "Slider moved to new position."
    | newPosition |
    newPosition := aPane position.
    newPosition = transactionIndex ifTrue: [^self]. "no change"
    self canDiscardWorkingTransaction
        ifTrue: [self cacheTransactionAt: newPosition; update]
        ifFalse: [self updateSlider: aPane "to cached values"]
```

To decide if we can move to the new transaction, we have to determine if the working transaction has been modified. If it has, we could just discard the changes. But if we want to save the changes, we should only permit the save if everything is valid.

```
canDiscardWorkingTransaction
    "Validate the working transaction and prompt for save if changes were made.
    Return whether or not the working transaction can be discarded."
    | result |
    workingTransaction = transaction ifTrue: [^true].
    result := MessageBox
        yesNoCancelTitled: 'Please Confirm' text: 'Save transaction?'.
    result isNil ifTrue: [^false "cancel and don't save"].
    result == #yes ifTrue: [
        self isWorkingTransactionValid ifFalse: [^false].
        self saveWorkingTransaction].
    ^true
```

We consider the working transaction to be valid if each pane is valid. We can determine if a pane is valid by validating it all over again.

```
isWorkingTransactionValid
    "Validate all the panes. Return whether or not successful."
    self mainView children do: [:aPane |
        (self isPaneContentsValid: aPane) ifFalse: [
            MessageBox message: 'Transaction data incorrect'.
            aPane setFocus.
            ^false]].
    ^true

isPaneContentsValid: aPane
    "Returns whether or not the pane passes the validation test."
    ^self validatePane: aPane
```

We have already seen method **cacheTransactionAt:** which simply obtains a new working transaction (repeated below for convenience). Method **update** simply asks each pane to **update** — the corresponding #getContents handlers will make the user interface reflect the contents of the working transaction.

```
cacheTransactionAt: index
    transactionIndex := index.
    transaction := transactionIndex = 0
        ifTrue: [Transaction new]
        ifFalse: [account at: transactionIndex].
    workingTransaction := transaction copy.
update
    "Make all panes in the window up-to-date."
    self mainView children do: [:aPane | aPane update]
```

6.9 Account and Transaction Processing

A typical account operation, like **Open** from the menu bar, can be handled with a method such as the following. Note that we take advantage of the file dialog which is built-in to Smalltalk.

```
openAccount
  "Open an existing account."
    | dialog file |
    self canDiscardAccount ifFalse: [^self].
    dialog := FileDialog new openFile.
    (fileName := dialog file) isNil ifTrue: [^self]. "user cancelled"
    file := File pathNameReadOnly: fileName.
    account := Compiler evaluate: file contents.
    file close.
    self cacheTransactionAt: account size; update
```

Similarly, a corresponding transaction initiated by button **New** or **Cancel** at the bottom of the account manager user interface might be handled as follows. Clearly, **newTransaction**: (**cancelTransaction**:) would be the handler for respective **#clicked** events.

```
newTransaction: aPane
    "Save the working transaction, if needed, and create a new one if its OK."
    self canDiscardWorkingTransaction ifFalse: [^self].
    self cacheTransactionAt: 0; update

cancelTransaction: aPane
    "Start all over again from the saved transaction."
    workingTransaction := transaction copy.
    self update
```

Other account and transaction operations can be done in a similar way.

6.10 Conclusions

Clearly, interface builders substantially simplify the task of configuring and laying out a new interface. But that's only a small part of building a new application. For this application, we spent at least six times longer implementing the desired functionality. So interface builders do not eliminate the need for experienced and knowledgeable programmers. On the other hand, this ratio would have been much different if we had had to produce the layout and pane construction code by hand.

One of the most useful features of the user interface builder was the capability to generate a new user interface, save it as an actual application, leave the builder permanently, and weeks later re-invoke the builder on the existing application and have it all work properly. Additionally, although we didn't use custom panes, the builder also supports it — something that we were able to take advantage of in other applications.

So would we use an interface builder again in a real application. Absolutely!! In fact, we now use it regularly.

7

Combining Modal and Non-modal Components to Build a Picture Viewer

7.1 Introduction

Over a period of several months, we watched a colleague develop an application interface that had a requirement for large numbers of iconic buttons and static pictures. A great deal of his time was spent importing color pictures from a Microsoft Windows paint program through the clipboard, finding that minor picture adjustments were needed, moving the pictures back to the paint program, and repeating the cycle.

There were several annoyances in this cycle. Since we had many dictionaries of such pictures, the picture to be updated had to be located, often by inspecting many candidates and displaying them by sending each an explicit display message to get a visual check. Next, care had to be taken to place a *copy* of the picture on the clipboard because the operation that moved the bits into the clipboard ultimately destroyed (released) the picture when a new picture was subsequently placed in the clipboard. Of course, if you could be guaranteed that the transfer was actually going to be successful, you could avoid making a copy. When the clipboard picture was successfully pasted into the paint program, it was necessary to come back to

Smalltalk to explicitly release the original picture because Smalltalk keeps handles into operating system memory where the bits are actually kept. Coming back the other way is much simpler because a new picture is created in the process.

What makes the process painful is that you have to continually execute bits and pieces of code that are kept, say in a special workspace. Every now and then, this code is discarded, sometimes deliberately and sometimes accidentally, and must be regenerated.

What was needed was a simple picture browser (see Figure 7.1) that supported these operations transparently. The browser we describe is based on an original design by Wayne Beaton but has undergone substantial modifications. In particular, the new design subscribes to the usual editing paradigm whereby a user is always editing a *copy* rather than the original. It also makes use of modal dialog boxes for opening and saving information. The modal dialog boxes and the browser, which we call the picture viewer, were all developed with Objectshare Systems' Window Builder.

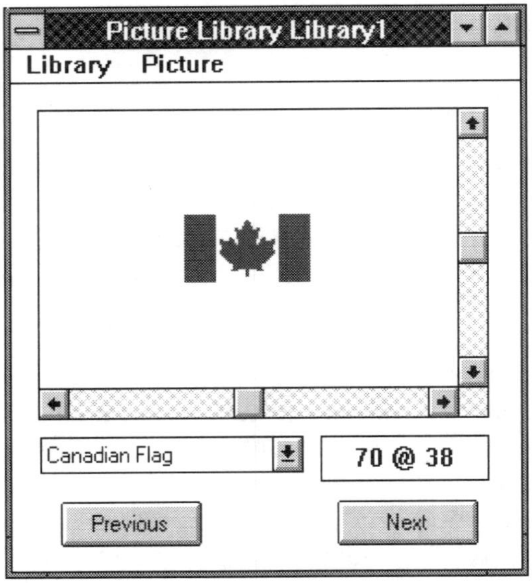

Figure 7.1 — The picture viewer.

7.2 Designing the Picture Viewer

The picture viewer is designed to keep track of a number of different picture libraries that it maintains in a class variable called PictureLibraries — a dictionary in which the key is the name of the library and the value is another dictionary of pictures keyed by the picture name. Although we haven't done it, it would be possible to save this library on disk using the object filer facilities that we made use of in Chapter 3.

In a typical session with the viewer, a user might open an existing library using **Open...** in the **Library** menu (see Figure 7.2). Next, he might look at the pictures it contains by clicking on the **Next** (or **Previous**) buttons. The name of the picture is displayed in the combo box while its extent is displayed to the right. It is also possible to go directly to a specific picture by selecting the appropriate name in the combo box.

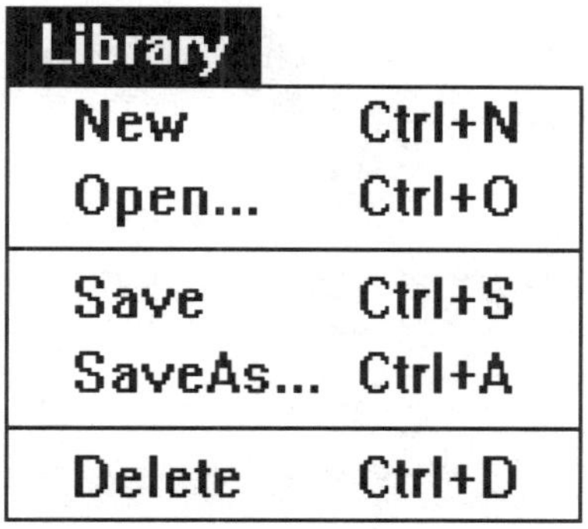

Figure 7.2 — The Library menu.

To copy a picture into the clipboard or paste the clipboard over an existing picture, the **Copy** or **Paste** operation respectively in the **Picture** menu can be used (see Figure 7.3). Menu command **New...** requires a prompt for the name of the picture; it produces an empty picture which can subsequently be pasted over.

Figure 7.3 — The Picture menu.

7.3 Providing Appropriate Modal Dialog Boxes

The original implementation of the picture viewer used simple prompters for reacting to **Open...** and **SaveAs...** in the **Library** menu. To improve on this, we used the Window Builder to design two dialog boxes as shown in Figures 7.4 and 7.5.

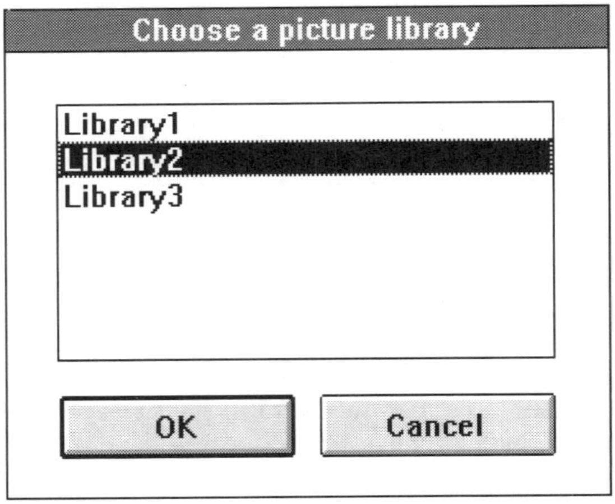

Figure 7.4 — The Open… dialog box.

Initially, these dialog boxes were specifically designed for the picture viewer but it quickly became apparent that little work had to be done to make them more generally useful. We called them ListQueryDialog (for picking and choosing an arbitrary element of a list) and ListExtensionDialog (for picking and choosing as before but also permitting the new element to be supplied by typing it). See Listings 7.1 and 7.2 for details of our implementation. The corresponding example class methods illustrate how they might be used.

Figure 7.5 — The SaveAs… dialog box.

Listing 7.1 — Class ListQueryDialog.

class	ListQueryDialog
superclass	WindowDialog
instance variables	result list title
pool dictionaries	ColorConstants
	WBConstants

class methods

examples

```
example1
    "ListQueryDialog example1"
    ^ListQueryDialog new
        openOn: #('red' 'green' 'blue')
        title: 'Choose a color'
```

```
WindowBuilder compatibility

wbCreated
    ^true

instance methods

opening

openOn: aCollection title: aString
    list := aCollection.
    title := aString.
    ^self open result

open
    "*** Code not shown ***"

result
    ^result

top pane event handling

opened: aPane
    "The #opened event handler for the window."
    self labelWithoutPrefix: title.
    (self paneNamed: 'listPane')
        contents: list;
        selectIndex: (list isEmpty ifTrue: [0] ifFalse: [1]);
        setFocus

list pane event handling

selectListEntry: aPane
    "Assumes the list entry is already selected."
    self ok: nil

button pane event handling

cancel: aPane
    result := nil.
    self close

ok: aPane
    result := (self paneNamed: 'listPane') selectedItem.
    self close
```

A **modal** window prevents users from carrying on in an application until a response is provided. Whether a window is to be modal or not is as simple as clicking a check box in the builder. The dialog box was designed to respond to four events:

- the top pane's **#opened** event which has to place the list of items in the list pane.
- the list pane's **#doubleClickSelect** event which doubles for a click on the **OK** button.
- the **OK** and **Cancel** buttons' **#clicked** event which respectively set the value of the **result** instance variable to the item selected in the list pane or nil.

When an **open** message is sent to this list query dialog (see method **openOn**:), execution is temporarily suspended until the dialog window is closed. Once it is closed, execution resumes and the next message (in this case **result**) is sent to the closed dialog window for an answer. In our case, we designed this method to return the contents of the instance variable "result" which is set prior to closing the dialog window. Any other message could have been used in place of **result**; i.e., there is no particular significance to the actual name chosen — it is not "built-in to the system."

The dialog box for class ListExtensionDialog was obtained by adding two more panes to the ListQueryDialog window: a static text pane (called subtitlePane) and an entry field (called namePane). A new **openOn**: method was designed to provide the additional subtitle information.

An additional handler, method **selectListEntry**:, for event **#select** in the list pane was added to ensure that the selected list element was inserted into the entry field. Selecting an element didn't require a handler in the previous dialog box because the selected element was retrieved only when the **OK** button was pressed (or, equivalently, when the item was double clicked). Of course, even though there was no handler, the list element was still selected as the user clicked on it in the list pane.

Listing 7.2 — Class ListExtensionDialog.

class	ListExtensionDialog
superclass	ListQueryDialog
instance variables	subtitle
pool dictionaries	ColorConstants
	WBConstants

```
class methods

examples

example1
    "ListExtensionDialog example1"
    ^self new
        openOn: #('red' 'green' 'blue') title: 'Choose a color' subtitle: 'Color name:'

WindowBuilder compatibility

wbCreated
    ^true

instance methods

instance initialization

openOn: aCollection title: aString subtitle: anotherString
  subtitle := anotherString.
  ^self openOn: aCollection title: aString

opening

open
    "*** Code not shown ***"

top pane event handling

opened: aPane
    super opened: aPane.
    (self paneNamed: 'namePane')
        contents: (list isEmpty ifTrue: [''] ifFalse: [list first]).
    (self paneNamed: 'subtitlePane') contents: subtitle

list pane event handling

selectListEntry: aPane
    "Assumes the list entry is already selected."
    (self paneNamed: 'namePane') contents: aPane selectedItem
```

```
doubleClickSelectListEntry: aPane
    "Assumes the list entry is already selected."
    self selectListEntry: aPane.
    self ok: nil
```

button pane event handling

```
ok: ignore
    result := (self paneNamed: 'namePane') contents.
    self close
```

7.4 Smalltalk/V Extensions to Support the Viewer

To support the manipulation of the pictures conveniently, it was necessary to add an obviously missing method to class Bitmap; e.g., a deep copy operations as shown in Listing 7.3.

Listing 7.3 — Extensions to Class Bitmap.

```
class                                                    Bitmap

instance methods

copying

deepCopy
    | bitmap |
    bitmap := self class screenExtent: self extent.
    bitmap pen
        copyBitmap: self
        from: self boundingBox
        at: 0@0.
    ^bitmap
```

More fundamental and problematic was the fact that half-way through our implementation, we discovered that copy operations for dictionaries were incorrectly implemented. We were taking deep copies of libraries (dictionaries of bitmaps) and finding that releasing the bitmaps in the copy destroyed the originals as well! Our initial reaction was to implement our own private method that performed the copy correctly but we ultimately decided that a proper solution required a change to the system.

The problem stems from the fact that the original designers provided an implementor's view of the solution rather than a user's view. Intuitively, a shallow copy of an array provides a user with a new array sharing the elements of the old. Moreover, changes to the new array don't affect the original. Similarly, a shallow copy of a dictionary should provide a user with a new dictionary sharing the keys and values of the old. Changes to the new dictionary should not affect the old (which was not the case). A deep copy is similar except that a shallow copy of the elements is made in the case of an array (a shallow copy of the keys and values in the case of a dictionary). Consequently, users expect to be able to physically modify the elements (keys and values) in the deep copy without affecting the corresponding elements (keys and values) of the original. As implemented in the original library, neither the shallow nor deep copy operation for dictionaries makes copies of the keys and values. The revised methods are shown in Listing 7.4.

Listing 7.4 — Extensions to Class Dictionary.

```
class                                        Dictionary

instance methods

copying

shallowCopy
    "Answer a copy of the receiver which shares the receiver keys and values (but not
    the same association objects)."
    | answer |
    answer := self species new.
    self associationsDo: [:element | answer add: element shallowCopy].
    ^answer

deepCopy
    "Answer a copy of the receiver with shallow copies of the keys and values (which
    requires a deep copy of the association objects)."
    | answer |
    answer := self species new.
    self associationsDo: [:element | answer add: element deepCopy].
    ^answer
```

Note the use of **species** in the code above. For most objects, method **species** returns the instance's class. For intervals, however, **species** returns class

Array. As a result, this permits users to execute something like following — clearly, we can't expect to get an interval back.

```
(1 to: 10 by: 2) collect: [:element | element squared]
```

7.5 Implementing the Picture Viewer

The picture viewer maintains two instance variables **libraryName** and **pictureName** (see Listing 7.5) for keeping track of the current library and picture names (either can be nil) and an instance variable **library** for maintaining a copy of the library being edited — a library is a dictionary containing pictures. By working on a copy, arbitrary modifications can be made without fear that the changes cannot be undone. The **update** operation can redisplay the complete user interface from these three variables. Instance variable **libraryChanged** ensures that we don't prompt the user for a save if no changes have been made. The remaining instance variables provide access to the important panes.

The picture viewer is similar to the modal dialog boxes in terms of the complexity of the panes and their interractions. What differentiates it from the dialog boxes is the extensive **Library** and **Picture** operations. To provide a flavor for the implementation, let's consider one sample from each group, say methods **libraryOpen** and **picturePaste**.

Method **libraryOpen** begins by prompting the user to save the current library if changes were made using **promptForSaveIfChanged**. If changes were made, this method in turn sends a **librarySave** message. If the library name is nil, this is converted to a **librarySaveAs** message (which prompts for a new name). We could pursue the **Save** (or **SaveAs**) messages further but it's more instructive to return to the **libraryOpen** method. Next, a dialog box is created to obtain the new library name from the user. If the user doesn't cancel (the name is nil if he does), the existing library (the working copy) must be discarded by explicitly releasing each bitmap (message **privateClearLibrary**:). The working library must be replaced by a copy of the library specified by the user. If there are pictures in the library, the name of the first picture in the sorted list is recorded; otherwise, nil is recorded. Once instance variables **libraryName** and **pictureName** are set, the **update** method can display all the required information in the user interface.

Method **picturePaste** implements the code for pasting over an existing picture. If a new picture is needed, the user should have performed a **New...** operation prior to the paste. The implementation begins by ensuring that there exists a selected picture for modification. Next, the old picture must be explicitly released before a new one can be obtained from the clipboard. The fact that the working library has been changed is recorded and the subset of the user interface affected is updated (in this case, just the picture portion).

The most worrisome problems with this specific application have to do with making sure bitmaps are released when they are no longer needed and ensuring that proper working copies of libraries are obtained; i.e., copies that duplicate the original bitmaps. Placing bitmaps in the clipboard also requires a copy because clipboard operation **setBitmap**: ultimately releases the bitmap when a new bitmap is added via a subsequent **setBitmap**: message.

Listing 7.5 — Class PictureViewer.

class	PictureViewer
superclass	ViewManager
instance variables	library libraryChanged libraryName pictureName
class variables	PictureLibraries
pool dictionaries	ColorConstants WBConstants

class methods

examples

example1
```
    "PictureViewer example1"
    self new open
```

example2
```
    "This example will prompt you to name a new picture. You will then see the
    crosshair cursor, implying that you should click-drag an area of the screen. This
    area of the screen will be captured as a picture and placed in the new picture
    viewer associated with the name you just entered."
    "PictureViewer example2"
    | aViewer |
    aViewer := self new open; pictureNew.
    Clipboard setBitmap: (Bitmap fromUser).
    aViewer picturePaste
```

class initialization

initialize

```
"PictureViewer initialize"
(PictureLibraries isKindOf: Dictionary) ifTrue: [self release].
PictureLibraries := Dictionary new
```

release

```
"PictureViewer release"
PictureLibraries do: [:library | library do: [:picture | picture release]]
```

library access and modification

libraries

```
"PictureViewer libraries"
^PictureLibraries
```

libraries: aDictionary

```
self initialize.
PictureLibraries := aDictionary
```

WindowBuilder compatibility

wbCreated

```
^true
```

instance methods

opening

open

```
"*** Code not shown ***"
```

library menu commands

libraryNew

```
self promptForSaveIfChanged.
self privateClearLibrary: library.
libraryName := pictureName := nil.
libraryChanged := false.
self update
```

libraryOpen

```
| name keys |
self promptForSaveIfChanged.
name := ListQueryDialog new
    openOn: PictureLibraries keys asSortedCollection
    title: 'Choose a picture library'.
name isNil ifTrue: [^self]. "User cancelled."
self privateClearLibrary: library.
library := (PictureLibraries at: name) deepCopy.
```

```
    libraryName := name.
    keys := library keys asSortedCollection.
    pictureName := keys isEmpty ifTrue: [nil] ifFalse: [keys first].
    libraryChanged := false.
    self update
librarySave
    libraryName isNil ifTrue: [^self librarySaveAs].
    self privateClearLibrary: (PictureLibraries at: libraryName).
    PictureLibraries at: libraryName put: library deepCopy.
    libraryChanged := false
librarySaveAs
    | name |
    name := ListExtensionDialog new
        openOn: PictureLibraries keys asSortedCollection
        title: 'Name new picture library'
        subtitle: 'Library Name'.
    name isNil ifTrue: [^self]. "User cancelled."
    self privateClearLibrary: (
        PictureLibraries at: name ifAbsent: [Dictionary new]).
    PictureLibraries at: name put: library deepCopy.
    libraryName := name.
    libraryChanged := false.
    self updateLabel
libraryDelete
    libraryName isNil ifTrue: [^self].
    (MessageBox confirm: 'Delete library ', libraryName) ifFalse: [^self].
    self privateClearLibrary: (PictureLibraries at: libraryName).
    PictureLibraries removeKey: libraryName.
    self privateClearLibrary: library.
    libraryName := pictureName := nil.
    self update
picture menu commands
pictureNew
    library isNil ifTrue: [^self].
    ^self privatePictureNewSized: 0@0
pictureCopy
    | picture |
    (picture := self picture) isNil ifTrue: [^self].
    Clipboard setBitmap: picture copy
pictureCut
    ^self pictureCopy; pictureDelete
```

```
picturePaste
    pictureName isNil ifTrue: [^self].
    (library at: pictureName) release.
    library at: pictureName put: Clipboard getBitmap.
    libraryChanged := true.
    self updatePicture
pictureDelete
    | names nameIndex |
    pictureName isNil ifTrue: [^self].
    (library at: pictureName) release.
    library removeKey: pictureName.
    names := (self paneNamed: 'pictureNamesPane') contents.
    nameIndex := (self paneNamed: 'pictureNamesPane') selectedIndex.
    pictureName := nameIndex > 1
        ifTrue: [names at: nameIndex - 1]
        ifFalse: [names size > 1 ifTrue: [names at: 2] ifFalse: [nil]].
    libraryChanged := true.
    self updatePictureNames; updatePicture
pictureRename
    | name picture |
    pictureName isNil ifTrue: [^self].
    name := self promptForName: 'new picture' in: library.
    picture := library at: pictureName.
    library removeKey: pictureName.
    library at: name put: picture.
    pictureName := name.
    libraryChanged := true.
    self updatePictureNames; updatePicture
top pane #opened and #close event handling
opened: aPane
    "Handler for the #opened event in the TopPane 'mainView'."
    library := Dictionary new.
    libraryName := pictureName := nil.
    libraryChanged := false.
    self update
closed: aPane
    "Handler for the #close event in the TopPane 'mainView'."
    self promptForSaveIfChanged.
    self privateClearLibrary: library.
    ^super close
```

button pane #clicked event handling

```
clickedNext: aPane
    self privateMovePictureByOffset: 1

clickedPrevious: aPane
    self privateMovePictureByOffset: -1
```

combo box #getContents event handling

```
getPictureName: aPane
    library isNil ifTrue: [^aPane contents: Array new].
    aPane
        contents: library keys asSortedCollection;
        selectItem: pictureName
```

combo box #select and doubleClickSelect event handling

```
selectPictureName: aPane
    pictureName := aPane selectedItem.
    self updatePicture
```

support operations

```
picture
    ^library at: pictureName ifAbsent: [nil]

promptForName: title in: aDictionary
    | name |
    name := Prompter prompt: 'Enter ', title, ' name or nothing to cancel' default: ''.
    (name isNil or: [name isEmpty]) ifTrue: [^nil]. "User changed his mind."
    (aDictionary keys includes: name)
        ifTrue: [
            (MessageBox confirm: 'Name already exists. Try again.')
                ifFalse: [^nil].
            ^self promptForName: title in: aDictionary]
        ifFalse: [^name]

promptForSaveIfChanged
    | name |
    libraryChanged ifFalse: [^self].
    name := libraryName isNil ifTrue: [''] ifFalse: [' ', libraryName].
    (MessageBox confirm: 'Changes made. Save Library', name, '?') ifFalse: [^self].
    self librarySave
```

updating

```
update
    self updateLabel; updatePictureNames; updatePicture
```

```
updateLabel
    self labelWithoutPrefix: 'Picture Library ',
        (libraryName isNil ifTrue: ['Untitled'] ifFalse: [libraryName])
updatePictureNames
    (self paneNamed: 'pictureNamesPane') update
updatePicture
    | picture offset picturePane pictureSizePane |
    picturePane := self paneNamed: 'picturePane'.
    pictureSizePane := self paneNamed: 'pictureSizePane'.
    picturePane pen isNil
        ifFalse: [picturePane pen deleteAllSegments; erase].
    pictureSizePane contents: ''.
    pictureName isNil ifTrue: [^self].
    picture := self picture.
    offset := (picturePane extent - picture extent) // 2.
    picturePane pen isNil ifFalse: [
        picturePane pen drawRetainPicture: [
            picturePane pen
                copyBitmap: picture from: picture boundingBox at: offset]].
    pictureSizePane contents: picture extent printString
private
privateClearLibrary: aDictionary
    aDictionary do: [:picture | picture release]; initialize: aDictionary size + 10
privateMovePictureByOffset: anInteger
    | names nameIndex newIndex |
    names := (self paneNamed: 'pictureNamesPane') contents.
    nameIndex := (self paneNamed: 'pictureNamesPane') selectedIndex.
    nameIndex isNil
        ifTrue: [nameIndex := anInteger positive
            ifTrue: [0]
            ifFalse: [names size + 1]].
    newIndex := nameIndex + anInteger.
    (newIndex between: 1 and: names size) ifFalse: [^self].
    pictureName := names at: newIndex.
    self updatePictureNames; updatePicture
```

```
privatePictureNewSized: extent
    | name picture |
    name := self promptForName: 'picture' in: library.
    name isNil ifTrue: [^nil]. "User changed his mind."
    picture := Bitmap screenExtent: extent.
    picture pen fill: ClrRed.
    library at: name put: picture.
    pictureName := name.
    libraryChanged := true.
    self updatePictureNames; updatePicture
```

7.6 Conclusions

Smalltalk programmers (ourselves included) have a tendency to be forever building new tools. With the aid of a window builder, such diversions can be easily justified since they don't take very much time and they often end up saving time in the long run.

Also, it should be clear that there is little difference between designing a dialog box and designing a non-modal window since the same tool can be used for designing both.

Tools that eliminate the problems inherent with the need for releasing bitmaps make it easier to avoid mistakes.

7.7 Acknowledgments

This chapter owes a great deal to Wayne Beaton who produced the first prototype. His interactive demonstration convinced us of the utility and simplicity of a picture viewer.

8

Pluggable Tiling Panes

8.1 Introduction

Our goal in this chapter is to explore high level Smalltalk events and event handlers by constructing a new class of panes with its own unique events. In previous chapters, we made use of built-in panes and provided event handlers for existing events. Here, we are more concerned with designing a new kind of pane that has its own unique events.

More specifically, we will design a **TilingPane** class for use in applications where it is advantageous to be able to divide a pane into arbitrary rectangular areas. Games and game boards come to mind since each square in a game can have interesting behavior associated with it. We will illustrate the use of such a pane by using it to implement a tic-tac-toe game.

First, we will very briefly explore the difference between low-level operating system events (Windows and OS/2 events) and higher-level Smalltalk events. We would like to deal solely with Smalltalk events but we will need to override a few of the low-level operating system event messages. Hence, it will be necessary to review and distinguish Smalltalk events from operating system events before proceeding to design our TilingPane class.

8.2 Windows (and OS/2) Events

In general, when a Smalltalk event is signalled via **event:**, the owner is informed of the event. Panes, however, are either directly or indirectly controlled by operating system events; i.e., Windows (or OS/2) events. These operating system events are kept internally as instances of InputEvent and passed along via special messages ***to the appropriate window*** by Notifier (the window and process manager). Such messages (whose parameters are low-level C structures) are prefixed by **wm** (for window manager). The corresponding methods reside in class **Window** from which all panes inherit — let's call them **pane messages** to avoid confusion. Some examples are shown in the left column of Figure 8.1.

These **low-level pane messages** get translated by the application window into **high-level pane messages** which are queued in CurrentEvents. Notifier sends these high-level messages ***to the appropriate pane*** for processing. Thus a window never gets to see actual input event objects.

Low-Level Pane Messages	High-Level Pane Messages
wmButton1down:with:	**button1Down**: aPoint **button1DownShift**: aPoint
wmMouseMove:with:	**button1Move**: aPoint **button2Move**: aPoint **mouseMove**: aPoint
wmChar:with:	**characterInput**: aCharacter **controlKeyInput**: aCharacter **virtualKeyInput**: anInteger
vmClose:with:	**close**

Figure 8.1 — Messages get translated by the application view manager.

The right column of Figure 8.1 shows that a single low-level pane message may have several possible high-level translations — depending on the context; e.g., **wmButton1down:with:** gets translated into **button1Down-Shift**: if the shift key is down, or simply **button1Down**: otherwise. See class Window for a full list of supported low-level and high-level messages. Currently, class Window provides a "do nothing" default for each high-level message like "**button1Down**: aPoint". Subclasses like GraphPane re-implement most of these high-level messages and send corresponding

Smalltalk window events (as opposed to operating system events) like #button1Down. A handler for a #button1Down event would have the form "**handlerForButton1Down**: aPane".

A new pane class should either inherit the methods for the high-level pane messages or re-implement them to provide new functionality. In our TilingPane (see Listing 8.2), we re-implemented

button1Down: aPoint
button1Up: aPoint
button1Move: aPoint
mouseMove: aPoint

to provide high level window events such as #enterTile, #selectTile, and #exitTile.

8.3 The Tic-Tac-Toe Game

We begin by implementing a version of the tic-tac-toe game that can be played without a user interface (see Listing 8.1). We will consider adding a user interface in the next section.

The game is played on a three by three board with coordinates of the form row@column where a row (or a column) is a number between 1 and 3. A new game is automatically initialized but it can be re-initialized at any time. Players are referenced by #X or #O. Either one may play first by executing

aGame **nextPlayer**: aPlayer

A move is played via

aGame **play**: aPlayer **at**: aCoordinate

It is an error to make an illegal move. Whether or not a move is legal can be determined before playing by sending the message

aGame **isLegalFor**: aPlayer **toPlay**: aCoordinate

The game may be queried at any time using the following:

aGame **nextPlayer**	(#X or #O)
aGame **gameOver**	(true or false)
aGame **winner**	(#X, #O or #NoOne)
aGame **winningLine**	(3 coordinates)

The game can be played without a user interface using prompters and pop-up menus. This is illustrated in class method **example1**.

Listing 8.1 — Class TicTacToeGame.

```
class                               TicTacToeGame
superclass                          Object
instance variables                  board lastPlayer winner
                                    winningLine
class variables                     WinningLines

class methods

instance creation

new
    ^super new initialize

class initialization

initialize
    "Generate all possible winning triples."
    "TicTacToeGame initialize"
    | square1 square2 square3 |
    WinningLines :=
        #((0 1 2) (3 4 5) (6 7 8) "rows"
        (0 3 6) (1 4 7) (2 5 8) "columns"
        (0 4 8) (6 4 2) "diagonals") collect: [:triple |
            square1 := triple first. square2 := triple at: 2. square3 := triple last.
            Array
                with: (square1 // 3)@(square1 \\ 3) + 1
                with: (square2 // 3)@(square2 \\ 3) + 1
                with: (square3 // 3)@(square3 \\ 3) + 1]

examples

example1
    "Play the game directly (all interractions are through simple prompters and dialog
    boxes)."
    "TicTacToeGame example1"
    | aGame response |
    aGame := TicTacToeGame new.
    aGame nextPlayer:
        ((MessageBox confirm: 'Does the X player want to start?')
            ifTrue: [#X]
            ifFalse: [#O]).
```

```
[aGame gameOver] whileFalse: [
    response := Prompter
        prompt: 'Player ', aGame nextPlayer,
            ', please provide the next board coordinate' "as a point"
        defaultExpression: '1@1'.
    (aGame isLegalFor: (aGame nextPlayer) toPlayAt: response)
        ifTrue: [aGame play: (aGame nextPlayer) at: response]
        ifFalse: [
            (MessageBox confirm: 'Bad move, do you want to continue?')
                ifFalse: [^self]]].
"The game is over"
Menu message: (aGame winner == #NoOne
    ifTrue: ['It''s a tie']
    ifFalse: ['You win, player ', aGame winner])
```

instance methods

instance initialization

```
initialize
    board := (Array new: 9) atAllPut: #Empty; yourself.
    winner := nil.
    lastPlayer := #NoOne

nextPlayer: aPlayer
    (lastPlayer == #NoOne) & ((aPlayer == #X) | (aPlayer == #O))
        ifFalse: [self error: 'initialize with #X or #O only at the beginning'].
    lastPlayer := aPlayer == #X ifTrue: [#O] ifFalse: [#X].
    ^aPlayer
```

testing

```
gameOver
    "Returns true iff the game is over."
    self winner == #NoOne ifFalse: [^true].
    board do: [:square | square == #Empty ifTrue: [^false]].
    ^true

nextPlayer
    ^lastPlayer == #X ifTrue: [#O] ifFalse: [#X]

winner
    "Returns either #X, #O, or #NoOne."
    | coordinate1 coordinate2 coordinate3 square1 square2 square3 |
    "If the winner has been previously computed and cached, avoid recomputing."
    winner ~~ nil ifTrue: [^winner].
```

```
    "Otherwise, consider each possible winning line."
    WinningLines do: [:triple |
        coordinate1 := triple first.
        coordinate2 := triple at: 2.
        coordinate3 := triple last.
        square1 := self at: coordinate1.
        square2 := self at: coordinate2.
        square3 := self at: coordinate3.
        (square1 ~~ #Empty) & (square1 == square2) & (square2 == square3)
            ifTrue: [
                winner := square1.
                winningLine := Array
                    with: coordinate1
                    with: coordinate2
                    with: coordinate3.
                ^winner]].
    "There is no winner."
    ^#NoOne

winningLine
    ^winningLine

board manipulation

at: aCoordinate
    "The board subscripts are linearized to 3 * (row - 1) + column."
    ^board at: 3 * (aCoordinate x - 1) + aCoordinate y

at: aCoordinate put: aValue
    "The board subscripts are linearized to 3 * (row - 1) + column."
    ^board at: 3 * (aCoordinate x - 1) + aCoordinate y put: aValue

playing

isLegalFor: aPlayer toPlayAt: aCoordinate
    (aCoordinate x between: 1 and: 3) & (aCoordinate y between: 1 and: 3)
        ifFalse: [^false].
    (self at: aCoordinate) == #Empty ifFalse: [^false].
    self winner == #NoOne ifFalse: [^false].
    ^lastPlayer ~= aPlayer

play: aPlayer at: aCoordinate
    (self isLegalFor: aPlayer toPlayAt: aCoordinate)
        ifTrue: [self at: aCoordinate put: aPlayer]
        ifFalse: [self error: 'you can''t play at ', aCoordinate printString].
    lastPlayer := aPlayer
```

Method **initialize** which sets up class variable WinningLines is tricky. If we temporarily number the squares 0, 1, 2, 3, 4, 5, 6, 7, 8 where 0, 1, 2 is the first row; 3, 4, 5 is the second row; and 6, 7, 8 is the third, it is relatively simple to convert these numbers into coordinates. For example, 5 should have coordinates 2@3. To get these coordinates, first divide by 3, next obtain the remainder after dividing by 3, and finally add 1 to the result; e.g.,

(square1 // 3)@(square1 \\ 3) + 1	
⇒ (5 // 3)@(5 \\ 3) + 1	(substituting square1 for 5)
⇒ (1)@(2) + 1	(after dividing (//) and remaindering (\\))
⇒ (1@2) + 1	(simplifying)
⇒ 2@3	(after adding 1 to a point)

8.4 Making TicTacToe Interactive

From a user's perspective, we would like to provide an interface to the game as shown in Figures 8.2 and 8.3. In this interface, the squares highlight and de-highlight as the cursor is moved over them with the mouse down. If the mouse is released in an unused square, either an X or an O is drawn depending on whose turn it is to play. When there is a winner, a line is drawn across the winning squares.

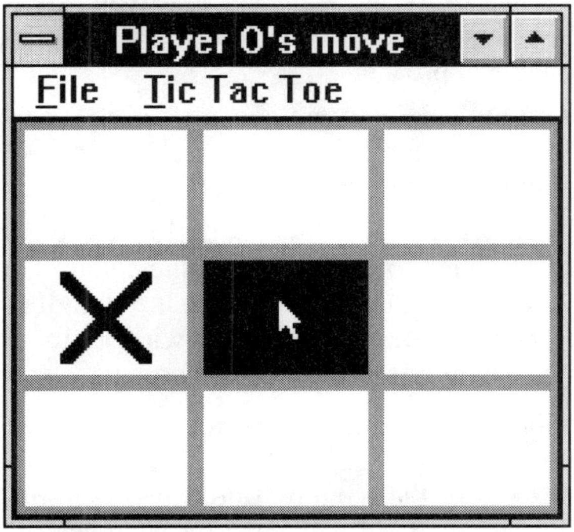

Figure 8.2 — A two-person tic-tac-toe game.

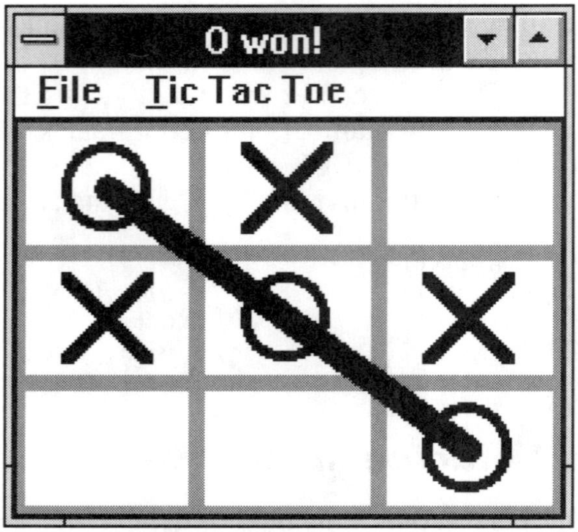

Figure 8.3 — A winning situation.

The important issue is *how to provide this functionality*. Three approaches are possible:

- Attempt to re-use existing panes? Not a good solution because there are none designed for this problem.
- Design our own specifically for the tic-tac-toe game — a reasonable approach.
- Attempt to design a more general facility that can be applied to a whole class of interface driven applications — an approach that is more in the OOP spirit of producing reusable code.

The second approach could be satisfied by designing a pane that is duplicated nine times for each of the nine squares in the game. We would have little difficulty having each pane handle the highlighting/de-highlighting of the squares and the drawing of the X's and O's. However, drawing the winning line at the end of the game is more problematic.

The third approach suggests we try for something simpler — perhaps one pane that, in addition to controlling the entire window, is able to handle different subareas of the window (the squares) individually. We want each subarea to be responsible for its own local processing (drawing the X's and O's) but we want to be able to override this with more global processing (the winning line). If these subareas are to play an important role in the evolving design, we should give them an appropriate name — so as not to confuse them with panes. We'll call them **tiles**.

So far, we are considering a pane whose role is to manage **tiles** — active areas in a window. If we are to design a facility that is more general than we actually need for this game, we will have to consider the functionality of the tiles in an application independent way. For example, the tiles could be applied to other games like checkers or chess. In any case, the tiles will ultimately have to interact with the application they are associated with.

Without reference to any specific application, we want the owner of the pane to be informed whenever mouse activity occurs over the tile. *What kind of activity?* Activity such as the following:

- **entering** the tile
- **exiting** the tile
- **changing** state over the tile (mouse button down to up or vice versa)

Moreover, we could differentiate between a mouse entering the tile (1) while no button is depressed, (2) while the left button is depressed, or (3) while the right button is depressed. This seems to lead to an excessive number of combinations. A compromise that is sufficiently general for most games might consider only activity in which the left button is depressed. Moving the mouse with no button depressed or with the right button depressed would be ignored. With this simplification, our application would be informed only when the left button is down and the mouse is

- **entering** the tile
- **exiting** the tile
- **releasing** over the tile

With this notion, the mouse (when depressed) can enter the tile and either exit or be released over the tile. Another variation, the one that we will finally use, is to ensure that entering and exiting are always paired. The third event is then changed to

- **selecting** the tile

A tile can then be **entered** (if the left mouse button is down). If the mouse moves off the tile without being released, an **exit** occurs. If it is released over the tile, both an **exit** (think of the mouse as having risen above the square) and a **selection** occurs. This way entering and exiting is always a matched pair — we can take advantage of this in a application; e.g., by having the handlers for these matched events simply reverse the color of the tile.

As an aside, the reader might note that interacting with a menu in Smalltalk conforms to this model in the following way:

- **entering** the menu item (highlights the item)
- **exiting** the menu item (de-highlights the item)
- **selecting** the menu item (dehighlights, hides, and executes the menu request)

Summarizing, we view **tiles** to be arbitrary rectangular areas that play the role of switches. Precisely what happens when a tile is entered, exited, or selected is the responsibility of the application. Since the application determines the result, the same pane (call them **tiling panes**) can be used to do completely different things in different applications. This is what is meant by the notion of **pluggable** panes — panes that can have application specific functions plugged in after the fact.

8.5 The Tiling Pane

As you can see from Figure 8.4, TilingPane was designed as a subclass of GraphPane to take advantage of its graphical facilities. TicTacToeWindow (discussed in the next section) is the application that provides a user interface to the game.

Listing 8.2 provides a complete listing of class TilingPane. To begin with, it supports three window events: #enterTile, #selectTile, and #exitTile. These events must be registered as supported events in a class method called **supportedEvents**. Failure to do so causes an error to be reported when a handler is associated with an event using **when:perform:** in an application window (we do this in TicTacToeWindow).

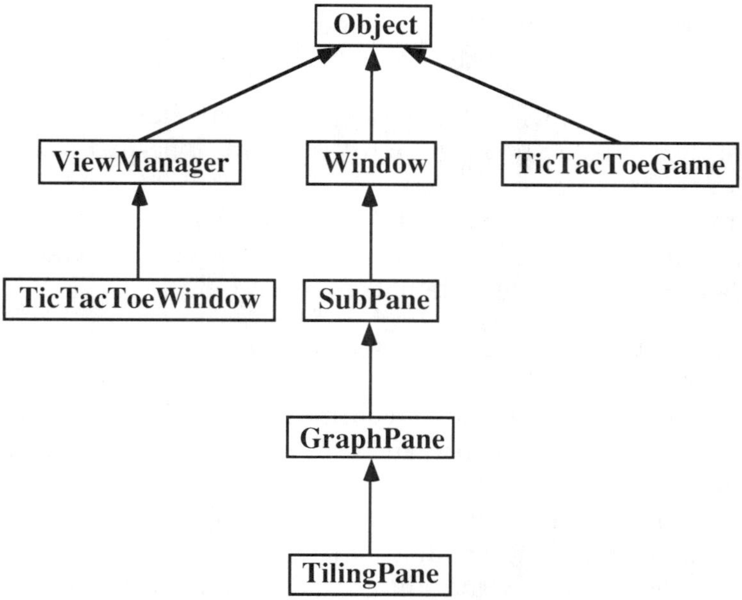

Figure 8.4 — Smalltalk/V game hierarchy.

These window events are generated by redefining pane messages **button1Down**:, **button1Up**:, **button1Move**: (moving when the left button is depressed), and **mouseMove**: (moving when no button is pressed). When the mouse button is pressed in a rectangle represented by a specific tile (method **button1Down**:), the #enterTile event is generated and the selected tile is recorded. If the mouse moves (methods **button1Move**: and **mouseMove**:), an #exitTile event is generated if the mouse moves out of the selected tile (if any). In the former case, an additional #enterTile event is generated if the mouse moves into a new tile which is now recorded as the selected tile. If the mouse button is released (method **button1Up**:) while in a selected tile, the #exitTile and #selectTile events are generated and the selected tile is unrecorded.

Initially, our code made the assumption that a **button1Up**: message, for example, was always preceded by a **button1Down**: (potentially interspersed with **button1Move**: messages). However, events generated by activity outside the window are never sent to the window, so if the mouse button is pressed outside and released inside (or vice versa), only the inside event is received by the window. The code shown appears more complex than necessary because it makes no such assumptions.

If the application using this pane (the owner) has no handler for a specific event (tested using message **handlesEvent**: inherited from class SubPane), the event is never generated and a default is executed. For entering and exiting (see methods **enterTile** and **exitTile**), the default behavior is to reverse the tile from black to white or vice versa. For selecting a tile (see method **selectTile**), the default is to do nothing.

From the perspective of a user of this class (an application window), handlers should be provided for events #getContents, #enterTile, #selectTile, and #exitTile. When the handler for #getContents is invoked, the application should provide the pane with the collection of tiles (the rectangles) using method **tiles**: in the tiling pane and additionally draw the tiles in the pane; i.e., do whatever is needed to make the tiling pane appear up-to-date. When the handlers for the other three events are invoked, the application can query the tiling pane for the associated tile using method **currentTile** and draw the appropriate tile. Drawing is achieved using the pane's pen.

Entering a tile corresponds to highlighting it, exiting to de-highlighting it, and selecting to choosing it. Entering and exiting are always matched up. Selecting only occurs after entering and exiting are matched; i.e., after pressing and releasing the mouse button over a tile. Note that the tiles in a tiling pane are arbitrary rectangles in coordinates that assume the pane's rectangle is 0@0 **extent**: 1@1. The rectangles are allowed to overlap and they need not cover the entire pane. However, we don't use this capability in our tic-tac-toe game.

Listing 8.2 — Class TilingPane.

class	TilingPane
superclass	GraphPane
instance variables	tiles selectedTile

class methods

event mechanism support

```
supportedEvents
    "Answer the Set of events that TilingPanes can notify their owners about."
    ^super supportedEvents
        remove: #button1DoubleClick;
        remove: #button1Down;
        remove: #button1DownShift;
        remove: #button1Move;
        remove: #button1Up;
        remove: #button2DoubleClick;
        remove: #button2Down;
        remove: #button2Move;
        remove: #button2Up;
        remove: #mouseMove;
        add: #enterTile;
        add: #exitTile;
        add: #selectTile;
        yourself
```

instance methods

low-level event handlers

```
button1Down: aPoint
    "The mouse is down in the pane at the cursor position. Enter the selected tile."
    (selectedTile := self activeTile: aPoint) isNil
        ifFalse: [self enterTile]

button1Move: aPoint
    "Every time the mouse moves in the pane with the left button down, notify the
    owner if a significant change has occurred; i.e., we crossed a tile boundary."
    | newTile |
    (newTile := self activeTile: aPoint) == selectedTile ifTrue: [^self].
    selectedTile isNil ifFalse: [self exitTile].
    (selectedTile := newTile) isNil ifFalse: [self enterTile]
```

```
button1Up: aPoint
    "The mouse button was released in the tile. Inform the owner."
    (selectedTile := self activeTile: aPoint) isNil
        ifFalse: [self exitTile; selectTile. selectedTile := nil]

mouseMove: aPoint
    "Every time the mouse moves in the pane, notify the owner if a significant
    change has occurred; i.e., we crossed a tile boundary."
    | newTile |
    (newTile := self activeTile: aPoint) == selectedTile ifTrue: [^self].
    selectedTile isNil
        ifFalse: [self exitTile. selectedTile := nil]
```

tiling actions

```
enterTile
    "Tell the application that the mouse has entered the tile. If no selector was
    provided by the application, defaults to reversing the tile."
    (self handlesEvent: #enterTile)
        ifTrue: [self event: #enterTile]
        ifFalse: [self reverseTile]

exitTile
    "Tell the owner that the mouse has left the tile. If no selector was provided by
    the application, defaults to reversing the tile."
    (self handlesEvent: #exitTile)
        ifTrue: [self event: #exitTile]
        ifFalse: [self reverseTile]

selectTile
    "Tell the owner that the mouse button has been released over the tile. If no
    selector was provided by the application, defaults to doing nothing."
    (self handlesEvent: #selectTile)
        ifTrue: [self event: #selectTile]
```

tiling support

```
activeTile: aPoint
    "Return the tile containing the cursor or nil if there is none."
    ^tiles isNil
        ifTrue: [nil]
        ifFalse: [
            tiles
                detect: [:aTile |
                    (self rectangle scaleTo: aTile) containsPoint: aPoint]
                ifNone: [nil]]

currentTile
    ^selectedTile
```

```
reverseTile
    "Invert the bits in the tile."
    | tileArea |
    tileArea := self rectangle scaleTo: selectedTile.
    tileArea := tileArea origin truncated corner: tileArea corner truncated.
    graphicsTool reverse: (tileArea intersect: self rectangle)
tiles: aCollectionOfRectangles
    tiles := aCollectionOfRectangles
```

8.6 The Tic-Tac-Toe Window

In Smalltalk/V for Windows (or V for OS/2), each application (in our case, TicTacToeWindow) is a subclass of ViewManager — see Figure 8.4. When an instance of a tic-tac-toe window is created (see method **initialize** in Listing 8.4), we create an instance of the tic-tac-toe game and construct a dictionary "tiles" that maps nine rectangles to board coordinates; coordinates 1@1 to 3@3.

It is also conventional for an instance of an application to create the required panes and start up when the user sends it an **open** or **openOn**: message. The application keeps track of all the information needed for the task including references to panes (if desired) that must inter-communicate. The pane references can be avoided using the change/update mechanism — see method **restart** to see how we referenced the tiling pane.

In our **open** method (see Listing 8.3), we first provide the application window with a special title (which changes as the game progresses) and we create one tiling pane. By default, graph panes (from which the tiling pane inherits) have scroll bars. The **style**: message with the proper parameter eliminates the scroll bars. For graph panes (and consequently tiling panes because of inheritance), the **stretch** can be either 0, 1, or 2 denoting "fixed size drawing," "variable size drawing but keeping the aspect ratio," and "variable size drawing independent of the aspect ratio" respectively. When the window is resized and the aspect ratio is kept, circles remain circles; otherwise, they become ellipses. In our case, we want our tic-tac-toe squares to grow and shrink proportional to the window whenever the window is resized — hence stretch parameter 2. After the handlers are set up, the window must be activated using **openWindow**.

The #getContents handler sets up the tiles in the tiling pane (just the keys in our variable called "tiles"), draws the background and the tiles, and the winner line if there is one. The #enterTile and #exitTile handlers just reverse the color of the tiles. The #selectTile handler does all the work. The method begins by asking the tiling pane for the selected tile — the relative rectangle. The corresponding game coordinate is obtained from the dictionary "tiles" which maps the relative rectangles to game coordinates via "tiles **at**: aPane **currentTile**". Then one step of the game is played — provided that it is legal. The modified tile is then redrawn and the label redisplayed. Mehtod **drawTile:on**: draws the tile in draw-retain mode so that automatic redisplay occurs when an obscured part of the window is uncovered. The pen drawing operations should be self evident.

Listing 8.3 — Class TicTacToeWindow.

```
class                    TicTacToeWindow
superclass               ViewManager
instance variables       game gameRectangle tiles
pool dictionaries        ColorConstants

class methods

examples

example1
    "TicTacToeWindow example1"
    self new open

instance methods

instance initialization

initialize
    "Set up the window."
    super initialize.
    "Set up the game."
    game := TicTacToeGame new.
    "Set up the tiles."
    tiles := Dictionary new.
    1 to: 3 do: [:row |
        1 to: 3 do: [:column |
            tiles
                at: (((column - 1)/3)@((row - 1)/3) extent: (1/3)@(1/3))
                put: row@column]]
```

opening

label

```
    "Answer the label for the game window."
    | theWinner |
    game gameOver ifFalse: [^'Player ', game nextPlayer, '''s move'].
    theWinner := game winner.
    theWinner == #NoOne ifTrue: [^'Nobody won.'].
    theWinner == #X ifTrue: [^'X won!'].
    theWinner == #O ifTrue: [^'O won!'].
    ^'Tic Tac Toe'
```

open

```
    "Start up a new game."
    | topPane |
    self
        labelWithoutPrefix: self label;
        owner: self.
    self addSubpane:
        (TilingPane new
            owner: self;
            stretch: 2;
            style: TilingPane noScrollBarsFrameStyle;
            when: #getContents perform: #tiles:;
            when: #enterTile perform: #enterOrExitTile:;
            when: #exitTile perform: #enterOrExitTile:;
            when: #selectTile perform: #selectTile:;
            when: #getMenu perform: #menu:).
    self openWindow
```

tiling pane change handling

enterOrExitTile: aPane

```
    "We will simply reverse the tile. Note: if this method is eliminated, the default will
    work the same way."
    | scaledRectangle |
    scaledRectangle := (gameRectangle scaleTo: aPane currentTile) insetBy: 3@3.
    aPane pen reverse: scaledRectangle
```

selectTile: aPane

```
    "A tile has been selected. Update the game and pane."
    | aCoordinate row column aTile |
    game gameOver ifTrue: [^self].
    aCoordinate := tiles at: (aTile := aPane currentTile).
```

```
    (game isLegalFor: game nextPlayer toPlayAt: aCoordinate)
        ifTrue: [game play: game nextPlayer at: aCoordinate]
        ifFalse: [
            6 timesRepeat: [
                aPane pen reverse: aPane rectangle.
                Time delayFor: 0.15].
                ^self].
    (game gameOver and: [game winner ~~ #NoOne])
        ifTrue: [self changed: #tiles:]
        ifFalse: [self drawTile: aTile on: aPane].
    self labelWithoutPrefix: self label
```

tiling pane pop-up menu handling

```
menu: aPane
    "Answer the menu for the TilePane."
    | aMenu |
    aMenu := Menu labels: 'restart' lines: #() selectors: #(restart).
    aMenu title: '~Tic Tac Toe'; owner: self.
    aPane setMenu: aMenu

restart
    "Restart the game."
    game initialize.
    self changed: #tiles:; labelWithoutPrefix: self label
```

tiling pane drawing

```
drawTile: aTile on: aPane
    "Draw a specified tile."
    | aCoordinate scaledRectangle tileType xBranchSize |
    aCoordinate := tiles at: aTile.
    scaledRectangle := (gameRectangle scaleTo: aTile) insetBy: 3@3.
    tileType := game at: aCoordinate.

    aPane pen drawRetainPicture: [
        aPane pen
            defaultNib: 4;
            place: scaledRectangle center truncated.
        xBranchSize := (scaledRectangle width min: scaledRectangle height) // 2.
        aPane pen blank: scaledRectangle.
        tileType == #X ifTrue: [
            aPane pen north; turn: 45.
            4 timesRepeat: [
                aPane pen go: xBranchSize; go: xBranchSize negated; turn: 90]].
        tileType == #O ifTrue: [
            aPane pen circle: xBranchSize * 3 // 4]]
```

```
drawWinnerLineOn: aPane
    "Draw a line from the centers of the outermost squares of the winning squares."
    | firstTile lastTile |
    firstTile := tiles keyAtValue: game winningLine first.
    lastTile := tiles keyAtValue: game winningLine last.
    aPane pen drawRetainPicture: [
        aPane pen
            defaultNib: 10;
            place: (gameRectangle scaleTo: firstTile) center;
            goto:  (gameRectangle scaleTo: lastTile) center]
tiles: aPane
    "Provide the tiling pane with a collection of relative rectangles for the tiles, setup
    the game rectangle if this is the first time through, and then draw the entire
    game using the pane's pen."
    | beginningTile endingTile |
    aPane tiles: tiles keys.      "Only the relative rectangles."
    gameRectangle isNil
        ifTrue: [gameRectangle := aPane rectangle].
    aPane pen
        deleteAllSegments;
        drawRetainPicture: [aPane pen fill: ClrDarkgray].
    tiles keysDo: [:aTile | self drawTile: aTile on: aPane].
    game winner == #NoOne ifFalse: [self drawWinnerLineOn: aPane]
```

8.7 Conclusions

We have briefly discussed the differences between operating system (Windows and OS/2) events (both low-level and high-level) and Smalltalk events, the former resulting in direct messages to panes and the latter resulting in messages that ultimately invoke event handlers in applications.

We have shown how we can design special panes with their own unique Smalltalk events. In our case, we were able to provide new Smalltalk events by redefining the high-level pane messages that are generated by lower-level **wm**... messages. It was possible to do this without understanding the details of the operating system events. In more complex applications, more knowledge will be needed since some of these **wm**.. messages may have to be redefined.

The pluggable tiling pane abstraction that we implemented can be reused in applications requiring the notion of active switches. Indeed, some readers may recognize active switches as the mechanism used by HyperCard®[1] to associate arbitrary code with buttons.

8.8 Acknowledgments

We would like to thank Nick Edgar who helped us prototype an early version of tiling panes and dispatchers in Smalltalk/V 286. Jon Hylands did the initial explorations in Smalltalk/V for Windows and helped port our tic-tac-toe game from the Smalltalk/V 286 version.

---

1 HyperCard is a registered trademark of Apple Computer, Inc.

9

Fuzzy Sets and Line Plots

9.1 Introduction

This chapter was inspired by Kurt Schmucker's [1] book ***Fuzzy Sets, Natural Language Computations, and Risk Analysis***. In this book, he describes and reviews the work on fuzzy sets, as pioneered by Lotfi Zadeh, and uses it as a basis for a fuzzy risk analyser. The approach is non-numeric in that it allows risk terminology like "very high," "rather low to medium," and "somewhat low" to be used.

Fuzzy sets are an active area of research in Artificial Intelligence (A.I.). Unfortunately, the notions of fuzzy sets are difficult to understand without pictorial tools that can help the user visualize the results of fuzzy operations on these sets.

Kurt's book is interesting because he provides detailed Pascal-like code for some of the simpler fuzzy operations. Our aim is two-fold: (1) to duplicate an illustrative subset of the notions and (2) to provide a facility for graphically displaying the sets. Smalltalk enables us to implement an operation that spans three pages of Pascal-like code in a dozen lines of

Smalltalk because of the support provided by the class library. It also provides us with powerful graphical facilities which we used for developing a simple line plot capability.

9.2 Fuzzy Sets

A fuzzy set is a set in which each member has an associated **degree of membership** — a real number between 0 and 1 inclusive; 0 indicating no membership and 1 indicating total membership. The degree of membership measures the extent that an element is in the set — 0.8 indicates that the element is 80% in the set.

Much of natural language is naturally fuzzy. For example, consider the following:

Paul is not very young.

Most Swedes are blond.

Pressure is low.

If X is a large number and Y is much larger than X, how large is Y?

In attempting to write natural language reasoners in A.I., it quickly becomes apparent that ordinary logic is not adequate to capture the imprecision in the statements. A comparison between standard logic and fuzzy logic taken from Zadeh [2] illustrates the distinction.

	Standard Logic	**Fuzzy Logic**
Predicates:	Even, odd, sad, ...	Tall, short, large, ...
Quantifiers:	None, all	Most, many, few, ...
Truth Values:	True, false	Very true, not quite true, ...
Probabilities:	0.3, 0.8, 0.99	Likely, unlikely, ...
Possibilities:	Possible, necessary	Quite possible, almost impossible
Consistency:	Yes, no	Mostly, a little, somewhat, ...

9.2.1 Young as a Fuzzy Set

Having said that such sets are best understood graphically, consider the problem of describing the imprecise term young. Is a ten year old young? How about a 25 year old or a 35 year old or a 60 year old? You might want to answer by saying: 10 — sure, 25 — yes, 35 — maybe (to some people perhaps), 60 — no. All of this can be summarized graphically as shown in Figure 9.1.

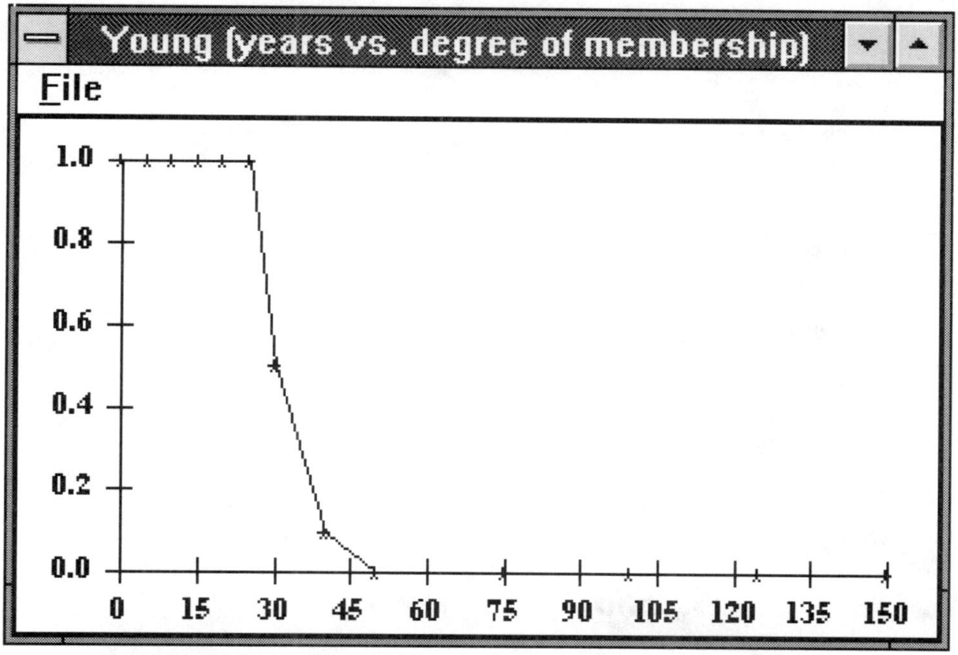

Figure 9.1 — The fuzzy set young described graphically.

Actually, the fuzzy set consists of integer ages with their corresponding degrees of membership. In particular, ages 0 to 25 have degrees of membership 1.0, age 30 has degree 0.5, 40 is 0.1, and 50 and above are 0.0.

9.2.2 Creating Fuzzy Sets

A fuzzy set can be viewed as a mapping from objects to degrees of membership. The simplest design is to inherit from class **Dictionary**. This allows us to inherit protocol for adding and removing elements from the set using **at:put:** and **removeKey:ifAbsent:**. From a design perspective, however, this is not the best approach because we don't think of fuzzy sets as dictionaries — fuzzy sets should be sets. Doing it properly would require the introduction of an AbstractSet class and a reorganization of the existing class hierarchy — something that wouldn't contribute to the main goal of this chapter. Listing 9.1 illustrates the class FuzzySet and provides a class method that constructs the fuzzy set **young**.

Listing 9.1 — Class FuzzySet.

```
class                                   FuzzySet
superclass                              Dictionary
instance variables                      "none"

class methods

instance creation

young
    "FuzzySet young"
    | fuzzySet |
    fuzzySet := self new.
    0 to: 25 by: 5 do: [:age | fuzzySet at: age put: 1.0].
    fuzzySet at: 30 put: 0.5; at: 40 put: 0.1.
    50 to: 150 by: 25 do: [:age | fuzzySet at: age put: 0.0].
    ^fuzzySet
```

9.2.3 Boolean Operations on Fuzzy Sets

The traditional operations **union**, **intersection**, and **complement** must be generalized for fuzzy sets. What does it mean to take the union of two fuzzy sets? It's not at all clear. However, the accepted definitions seem to be the following:

union ⇒ maximum memberships

intersection ⇒ minimum memberships

complement ⇒ 1 - memberships

For example, suppose object1 has membership 0.6 in set 1 and 0.8 in set 2. What degree of membership does object1 have in the union? Clearly, if one set believes its 0.6 and the other believes its 0.8, then someone believes its 0.8 — so 0.8 (the maximum) is a reasonable answer. Alternatively, if the degrees of memberships are taken to be the heights of a fixed width rectangle, the union is obtained by overlaying the two rectangles. The result is the maximum height. For intersection, the area common to both is the same as the miminum height rectangle. For complement of a single membership, it is the area above that is not used — since the sum of the two heights is one, the height of the complement is one minus the original membership.

Listing 9.2 provides methods for two querying operations and the three boolean operations. The querying operations are provided to solve a small problem. What is the difference between an element in the set with degree of membership 0 and an element that is not in the set? The answer should be *"they are the same."* Now suppose we have a set {a} where a has degree of membership 0.2. What is the complement of the set. The correct answer can only be determined if we know the universe from which the original set was constructed. If elements that could have been in {a} include a, b, and c (and only those elements), then the complement of the set is {a/0.8, b/1, c/1}. In this notation, a has degree of membership 0.8, b has 1 (because in the original set, it had membership 0), etc. Since we don't keep track of the set's universe, are we to assume that all objects not mentioned (literally, all possible Smalltalk objects) are in the complement. This is highly improbable and also impossible to implement. Our solution is to require all elements in the set's universe to be in the set — with membership 0 if considered absent.

To implement the three operations, it is convenient to include the sequencing operation **do**: that takes a two-parameter block. This **do**: permits the elements with their corresponding degree of membership to be obtained in some arbitrary order.

Listing 9.2 — Querying and boolean operations on fuzzy sets.

```
instance methods
querying operations
memberDegree: anObject
    "Given that anObject is in the set's universe, to what degree is it in?"
    ^self at: anObject ifAbsent: [self error: 'not in the set''s universe']
memberInUniverse: anObject
    "Is anObject in the set's universe?"
    self at: anObject ifAbsent: [^false].
    ^true
boolean operations
union: aFuzzySet
    "Returns a new set that is the union of self and aFuzzySet; i.e., the maximum
    degree of membership for each element in either set."
    | result newMembership |
    result := self deepCopy.
    aFuzzySet do: [:element :membership | newMembership :=
        membership max: (self at: element ifAbsent: [membership]).
        result at: element put: newMembership].
    ^result
intersect: aFuzzySet
    "Returns a new set that is the intersection of self and aFuzzySet; i.e., the minimum
    degree of membership for each element that is in both sets."
    | result newMembership selfMembership |
    result := self class new.
    aFuzzySet do: [:element :membership |
        selfMembership := self at: element ifAbsent: [nil].
        selfMembership isNil ifFalse: [
            newMembership := membership min: selfMembership.
            result at: element put: newMembership]].
    ^result
complement
    "Returns a new set that is the complement of self. Subtract each membership from 1."
    | result |
    result := self class new.
    self do: [:element :membership | result at: element put: 1 - membership].
    ^result
```

sequencing

```
do: aBinaryBlock
    "Permits use in the form aFuzzySet do: [:setElement :degreeOfMembership | ...]."
    self associationsDo: [:anAssociation |
        aBinaryBlock value: anAssociation key value: anAssociation value]
```

9.2.4 Complex Operations on Fuzzy Sets

Kurt's book defines several complicated fuzzy operations including four that we have implemented in Listing 9.3: **concentrate**, **dilate**, **intensify**, and **normalize**. Definitions are provided in the methods.

Listing 9.3 — Complex operations on fuzzy sets.

```
instance methods

complex operations

concentrate
    "Returns a new set that is the concentration of self. A fuzzy set is concentrated by
    squaring each degree of membership."
    | result |
    result := self class new.
    self do: [:element :membership | result at: element put: membership squared].
    ^result

dilate
    "Returns a new set that is the dilation of self. A fuzzy set is dilated by taking the
    square root of each degree of membership."
    | result |
    result := self class new.
    self do: [:element :membership | result at: element put: membership sqrt].
    ^result

intensify
    "Returns a new set that is self intensified. A fuzzy set is intensified by squaring
    and doubling each degree of membership less than 0.5; otherwise, the same
    operation is applied to the complement and the complement of the result is used."
    | result newValue |
    result := self class new.
    self do: [:element :membership |
        newValue := membership <= 0.5
            ifTrue: [2 * membership squared]
            ifFalse: [1 - (2 * (1 - membership) squared)].
        result at: element put: newValue].
    ^result
```

```
normalize
    "Returns a new set that is self normalized. A fuzzy set is normalized by dividing
    each membership by the maximum membership."
    | maximum result |
    "Find maximum membership."
    maximum := 0.
    self do: [:element :membership | maximum := maximum max: membership].

    "Divide each member's membership by the maximum."
    result := self class new.
    self do: [:element :membership | result at: element put: membership / maximum].
    ^result
```

It is more intuitive to provide graphical descriptions of the complex operations. For example, consider the fuzzy sets **bell** and **halfBell** in Listing 9.4 — they were constructed for their shape, not for their acoustic interpretation.

Listing 9.4 — Fuzzy sets bell and halfBell.

```
class                                                    FuzzySet

class methods

instance creation

bell
    "FuzzySet bell"
    self new
        at: 0 put: 0;
        at: 1 put: 0.1;
        at: 2 put: 0.2;
        at: 3 put: 0.5;
        at: 4 put: 0.8;
        at: 5 put: 1;
        at: 6 put: 0.8;
        at: 7 put: 0.5;
        at: 8 put: 0.2;
        at: 9 put: 0.1;
        at: 10 put: 0;
        yourself
```

```
halfBell
    "FuzzySet halfBell"
    | result |
    result := self new.
    self bell do: [:element :membership | result at: element put: membership / 2.0].
    ^result
```

Figures 9.2 through 9.4 illustrate the complex operations **concentrate**, **dilate**, and **intensify** on **bell**; Figure 9.5 illustrates the **normalize** operation on **halfBell**. Intuitively, **concentrating** a set decreases the membership (the less its in the set, the more it is decreased). **Dilation** is the opposite of **concentation**. **Intensification** is a combination of concentration and dilation — it heightens the contrast between the elements that are more than half in (by increasing their degree) and the elements that are less than half in (by decreasing their degree). Finally, **normalization** simply scales the values so that the maximum value is 1. As shown in Figure 9.5, normalizing a half bell gives you back the bell (or a close approximation).

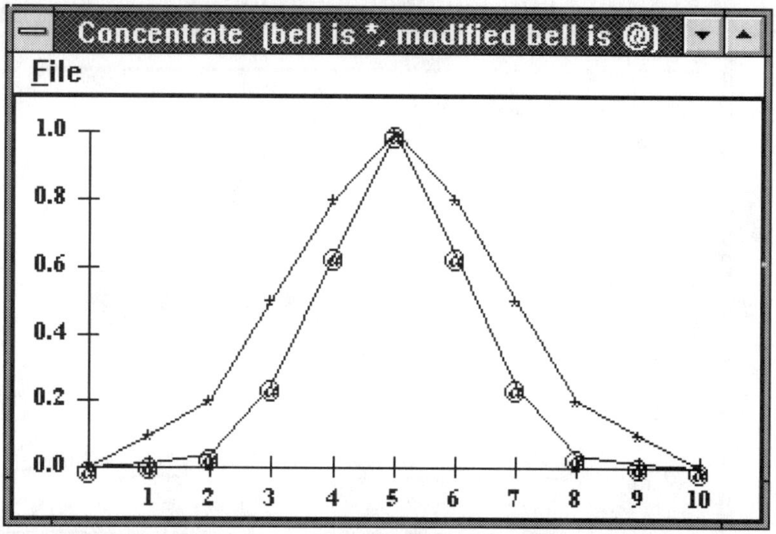

Figure 9.2 — Illustrating operation **concentrate** on a bell curve.

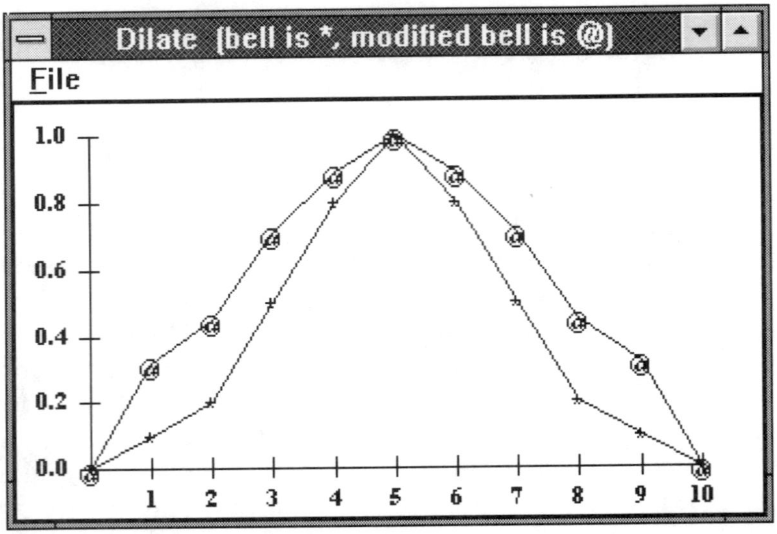

Figure 9.3 — Illustrating operation **dilate** on a bell curve.

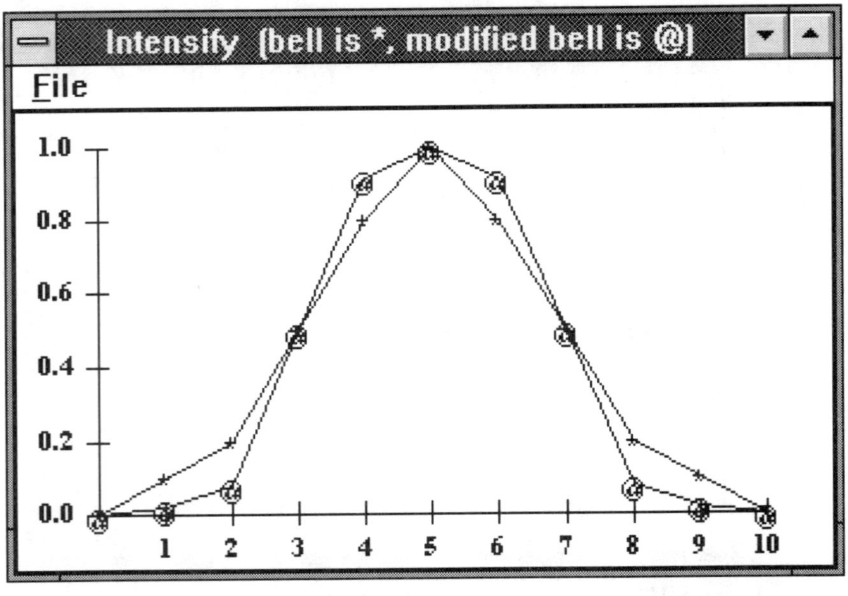

Figure 9.4 — Illustrating operation **intensify** on a bell curve.

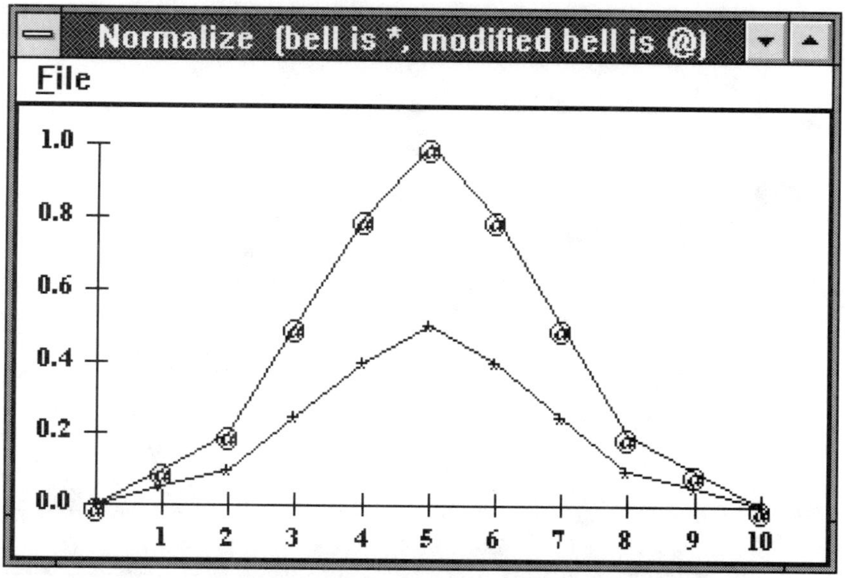

Figure 9.5 — Illustrating operation **normalize** on a half-bell curve.

9.2.5 Quantifiers on Fuzzy Sets

The complex operations can be used to implement quantifiers on the fuzzy sets; i.e., linguistically motivated operations. We provide five: **not**, **pretty**, **slightly**, **sortOf**, and **very**. We can apply them successively to obtain more complex operations; e.g., 'FuzzySet **tall very not**' would give us the set "not very tall." The definitions are taken from Lakoff [3]. In general, these and similar definitions reflect the whims of the designers. The hope is that they capture the intuitive meanings understood by people, but there is no theory to ensure that this is the case.

Figure 9.6 illustrates these quantifiers applied to fuzzy set **tall** (see the window title for the legend). Listing 9.5 provides methods that implement them.

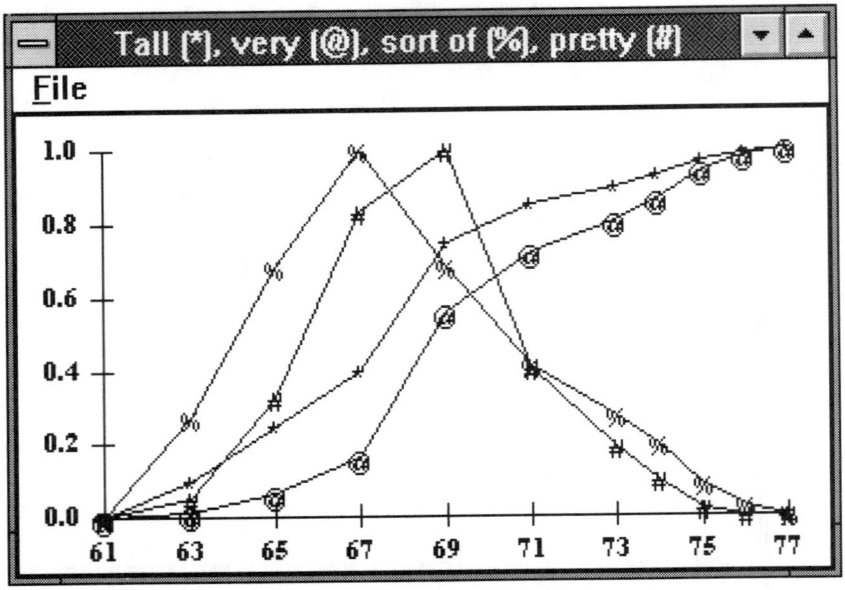

Figure 9.6 — Fuzzy quantifiers on tall.

Listing 9.5 — Linguistic quantifiers on fuzzy sets.

```
class                                              FuzzySet

class methods
instance creation

tall
    "FuzzySet tall"
    ^self new
        at: 61 "5 feet 1  inches" put: 0;
        at: 63 "5 feet 3  inches" put: 0.1;
        at: 65 "5 feet 5  inches" put: 0.25;
        at: 67 "5 feet 7  inches" put: 0.4;
        at: 69 "5 feet 9  inches" put: 0.75;
        at: 71 "5 feet 11 inches" put: 0.85;
        at: 73 "6 feet 1  inches" put: 0.9;
        at: 74 "6 feet 2  inches" put: 0.93;
        at: 75 "6 feet 3  inches" put: 0.97;
        at: 76 "6 feet 4  inches" put: 0.99;
        at: 77 "6 feet 6  inches" put: 1;
        yourself
```

instance methods

quantifiers

not
```
    "FuzzySet tall not"
    ^self complement
```

pretty
```
    "FuzzySet tall pretty"
    ^(self intensify intersect: self concentrate intensify not) normalize
```

slightly
```
    "FuzzySet tall slightly"
    ^(self intersect: self very not) normalize
```

sortOf
```
    "FuzzySet tall sortOf"
    ^(self dilate intensify intersect: self not dilate intensify) normalize
```

very
```
    "FuzzySet tall very"
    ^self concentrate
```

9.3 LinePlots — Displaying Fuzzy Sets

The figures shown in this chapter were all displayed using a special class **LinePlot**. To plot fuzzy sets, it is sufficient to provide a sequence of x-coordinate values and a corresponding sequence of y-coordinate values. For fuzzy sets in which the elements are numerical, line plots could be provided with the keys and values in correspondence. Rather than use the dictionary protocol, we added FuzzySet protocol to obtain the **domain** and **range**.

Listing 9.6 — Operations domain and range on fuzzy sets.

class FuzzySet

instance methods

accessing

domain
```
    "The domain for a set consists of the objects in the set. Returns a sorted collection
    of these objects."
    ^self keys asSortedCollection
```

range
"The range for a set consists of the degree of membership of the objects in the set. Returns a collection of member degrees in the same sorted order as the domain."
^self **domain asArray collect**: [:key | self **at**: key]

The LinePlot class must support multiple plots (see Figure 9.6). The protocol we wish to provide is best illustrated through the examples shown in Figures 9.1 through 9.6. As Listing 9.7 indicates, sequences of domains and ranges along with a **marker** — a special character used to label the line plotted — are provided. Another approach would have been to use color. The rest of the information is optional. The **x-View** and **y-View** specify the total viewing area in terms of user coordinates — this includes the areas for the axes, the tick marks and the numbers displayed along the tick marks. The axes are specified by specifying the x-range, the y-range, and the intersection point — typically the origin. The tick marks are specified as a collection of values in user coordinates.

Listing 9.7 — Plotting fuzzy sets.

```
class methods
examples
example1
    "Plots fuzzy set young without detailed plot specifications."
    "FuzzySet example1"
    | fuzzySet |
    fuzzySet := FuzzySet young.
    LinePlot new
        add: fuzzySet domain and: fuzzySet range marker: $*;
        plot
example2
    "Plots fuzzy set tall without detailed plot specifications."
    "FuzzySet example2"
    | fuzzySet |
    fuzzySet := FuzzySet tall.
    LinePlot new
        add: fuzzySet domain and: fuzzySet range marker: $*;
        plot
```

```
example3
    "Plots fuzzy set young with detailed plot specifications."
    "FuzzySet example3"
    | fuzzySet |
    fuzzySet := FuzzySet young.
    LinePlot new
        add: fuzzySet domain and: fuzzySet range marker: $*;
        label: 'Young (years versus degree of membership)';
        xView: 0@150 yView: 0.0@1.0;
        xAxis: 0@150 yAxis: 0@1 origin: 0@0;
        xTicks: (0 to: 150 by: 15);
        yTicks: (0 to: 1 by: 0.2);
        plot
example4
    "Plots fuzzy set tall with detailed plot specifications."
    "FuzzySet example4"
    | tall next |
    tall := FuzzySet tall.
    LinePlot new
        add: tall domain and: tall range marker: $*;
        add: (next := tall very) domain and: next range marker: $@;
        add: (next := tall sortOf) domain and: next range marker: $%;
        add: (next := tall pretty) domain and: next range marker: $#;
        label: 'Tall (*), very tall (@), sort of tall (%), pretty tall (#)';
        xView: 61@77 yView: 0@1;
        xAxis: 61@77 yAxis: 0@1 origin: 61@0;
        xTicks: (61 to: 77 by: 2);
        yTicks: (0 to: 1 by: 0.2);
        plot
```

9.3.1 Transformations — Resizing Line Plots

To simplify the conversion from user coordinates; e.g., y-coordinates ranging from 0.5 through 0.9, to window coordinates; e.g., 300 to 200, we introduced a transformation class. This transformation class (see Listing 9.8) keeps track of a scale and a translation.

The basic aim is to be able to take a point in user coordinates (say a point in rectangle1 of Figure 9.7) and transform it to the corresponding point in rectangle2.

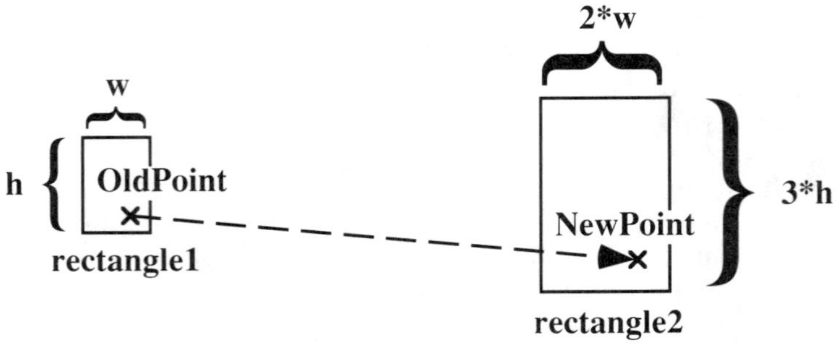

Figure 9.7 — Transforming a point in rectangle1 to a point in rectangle2.

To achieve this coordinate transformation, both a scale and a translation are required. So we could either write

NewPoint = (OldPoint * Scale) + Translation

or

NewPoint = (OldPoint + Translation) * Scale.

Both can be made to work, but the first scheme is more conventional.

The scale can be determined from the rectangle widths and heights; i.e., we want a scale that makes the following true:

(rectangle1 **width**) * scale = rectangle2 **width**.

The same applies for the height. Hence, in two dimensions, this generalizes to

(rectangle1 **extent**) * scale = rectangle2 **extent**

or

scale = rectangle2 **extent** / rectangle1 **extent**.

If, for example, the extent of the original rectangle was 10@12 (10 pixels wide and 12 pixels high) and the extent of the final rectangle was to be 20@36, the scale would have to be (20@36) / (10@12) = (2@3). The translation can be determined from the original equation by substituting any two corresponding points in the two rectangles; e.g., the top left corners or the midpoints, and using the equation

Translation = NewPoint - (OldPoint * Scale).

For example, if the top left corner of rectangle1 (oldPoint) was 10@10 and the corresponding corner in rectangle2 (newPoint) was 100@0, the required translation (assuming a scale factor of 2@3) would be:

```
  (100@0) - ((10@10) * (2@3))
= (100@0) - (20@30)
= (80@-30)
```

In Smalltalk/V for OS/2, the above is sufficient for our purposes. In Smalltalk/V for Windows, however, the coordinate system for windows has increasing y directed downward (the top is zero). Since user coordinates have y values increasing upward, all graphs need to be flipped. The solution is to supply a negative y scale factor.

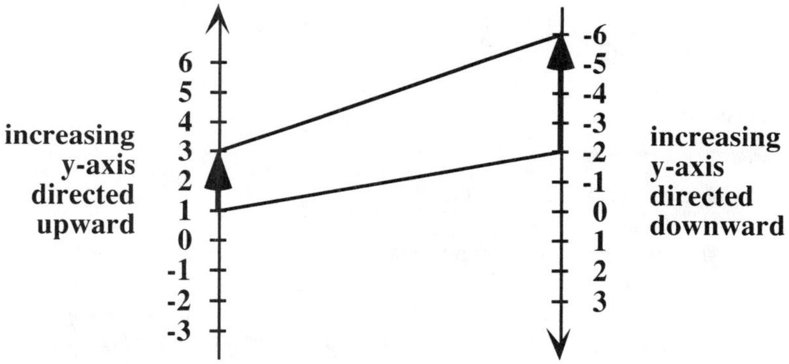

Figure 9.8 — Scaling y-coordinates by -2.

Consider drawing a vertical line segment by connecting y-coordinate 1 to y-coordinate 3 in a coordinate system for which y increases upward (see the left side of Figure 9.8). If we scale by -2, the successive y-coordinates become -2 and -6 respectively. If the points are plotted on a graph with y increasing downward (see the right side of Figure 9.8), the line segment from -2 to -6 is directed upward (as it should be). Of course, the line is in the negative region rather that the positive region, but a subsequent translation can move it down.

A solution, therefore, is to use a positive y-scale in Smalltalk/V for OS/2 and a negative y-scale in Smalltalk/V for Windows. The respective translations will be totally different in each case, but they will each be correct for their associated coordinate system. One way of doing this in a machine independent manner is to use

rectangle2 **rightTop** - rectangle2 **leftBottom**

rather than

rectangle2 **extent**.

The user coordinate system is never inverted so the extent is used to ensure positive values.

Listing 9.8 — Class Transformation.

```
class                                   Transformation
superclass                              Object
instance variables                      scale translation

class methods

instance creation

from: rectangle1 to: rectangle2
    | scale signedExtent |
    signedExtent := rectangle2 rightTop - rectangle2 leftBottom.
    ^self new
        scale: (scale := (signedExtent / rectangle1 extent) asFloat);
        translation: rectangle2 leftTop - (rectangle1 leftTop * scale)

instance methods

printing

printOn: aStream
    aStream nextPutAll: 'aTransformation scale: '.
    self scale printOn: aStream.
    aStream nextPutAll: ' translation: '.
    self translation printOn: aStream

transfomation

transform: aPointOrRectangle
    (aPointOrRectangle isKindOf: Point)
        ifTrue: [^(aPointOrRectangle * scale + translation) rounded]
        ifFalse: [^Rectangle
            leftTop: (aPointOrRectangle leftTop * scale + translation) rounded
            rightBottom: (aPointOrRectangle rightBottom * scale + translation)
                rounded]
```

accessing and modifying

scale
    ^scale

scale: aPoint
    scale := aPoint **asFloat**

translation
    ^translation

translation: aPoint
    translation := aPoint **asFloat**

9.3.2 The LinePlot Class

The LinePlot class (shown in Listing 9.9) could simply record the information provided; the xyView, xAxis, and yAxis as rectangles and the xTicks and yTicks as collections (normally intervals). Originally, xyView was entirely specified in user coordinates by specifying an x-range and a y-range; e.g., 1 to 10 for the x-range and 0.0 to 1.0 for the y-range. If a user wanted extra space on the left side (or the bottom), we had to specify a larger range; e.g., -1 to 10 rather than 1 to 10. But the plotting area is ultimately scaled to window coordinates. Since the width and height are scaled differently, it can be difficult to obtain equal amounts of white space on both the left side of the y-axis and the bottom of the x-axis.

A friendlier approach permits the user to specify this additional space in absolute screen pixels (window coordinates) by specifying an optional x-indent and y-indent. The implementation can then worry about determining what this absolute white space corresponds to in user coordinates. Of course, this cannot be done until the window opens because the actual window size is needed to work out the scale factor. One way of accommodating this is to delay to construction of the xyView rectangle until after the window opens. The needed information is, of course, supplied prior to opening the window. We simply construct a message which is stored in an instance variable "computeViewMessage" that is executed at the appropriate time. By default, this variable contains a message with selector **computeXYViewFromAxes** but this can be substituted by **computeXYViewFromxView**:**xIndents**:**y-View**:**yIndents**: if the user provides more specific view information.

Method **plot** does the real work. It constructs a window with a graph pane that draws the line plot as soon as a #getContents event is generated. This event is generated whenever a pane is out-of-date; e.g., when the window is first opened (automatic) or when an **update** message is sent to the pane (application driven).

The line and text drawing performed by method **displayOn**: can be studied to determine the details. Of interest are the special sequencing operations (control structures) like **pointCollectionsDo**:, **pointsDoFirst**:**rest**:, **xTicksDo**: and **yTicksDo**:.

Listing 9.9 — Class LinePlot.

```
class                   LinePlot
superclass              Object
instance variables      label transformation markers
                        pointCollections xyView
                        xAxis yAxis xTicks yTicks
                        pane computeViewMessage
pool dictionaries       WinConstants

class methods

instance creation

new
    ^super new initialize

instance methods

instance initialization

initialize
    "New line plots are pre-initialized."
    pointCollections := OrderedCollection new.
    markers := OrderedCollection new.
    label := ''.
    computeViewMessage := Message new
        receiver: self
        selector: #computeXYViewFromAxes
        arguments: #()
```

accessing and modifying

label
    ^label

label: aString
    label := aString

axes

xAxis
    "Returns the xAxis bounds as a rectangle. Compute it if not user supplied."
    xAxis **isNil ifTrue**: [self **computeAxes**].
    ^xAxis

yAxis
    "Returns the yAxis bounds as a rectangle. Compute it if not user supplied."
    yAxis **isNil ifTrue**: [self **computeAxes**].
    ^yAxis

xAxis: xRangePoint **yAxis**: yRangePoint **origin**: intersectionPoint
    "The user supplied data is used to construct a rectangle denoting the x- and y-axis."
    xAxis := Rectangle
        leftBottom: xRangePoint **x** @ intersectionPoint **y**
        rightTop: xRangePoint **y** @ intersectionPoint **y**.
    yAxis := Rectangle
        leftBottom: intersectionPoint **x** @ yRangePoint **x**
        rightTop: intersectionPoint **x** @ yRangePoint **y**

computeAxes
    "Used to determine default x and y-axis bounds from the plotting data. Assumes the axes cross at the minimum x and y values."
    | minimum maximum |
    self
        originalPointsDoFirst: [:point :marker | minimum := maximum := point]
        rest: [:point :marker |
            minimum := minimum **min**: point. maximum := maximum **max**: point].
    xAxis := Rectangle
        leftBottom: minimum **x**@minimum **y**
        rightTop: maximum **x**@minimum **y**.
    yAxis := Rectangle
        leftBottom: minimum **x**@minimum **y**
        rightTop: minimum **x**@maximum **y**

ticks

xTicks
    "Returns a collection of x-coordinates where tick marks are to be displayed. Use an empty collection if not user supplied."
    xTicks **isNil ifTrue**: [^#()] **ifFalse**: [^xTicks]

xTicks: aCollection
"Record the collection of x-coordinates where tick marks are to be displayed."
xTicks := aCollection

yTicks
"Returns a collection of y-coordinates where tick marks are to be displayed. Use an empty collection if not user supplied."
yTicks **isNil ifTrue**: [^#()] **ifFalse**: [^yTicks]

yTicks: aCollection
"Record the collection of y-coordinates where tick marks are to be displayed."
yTicks := aCollection

views

computeXYView
"Used to compute a default view rectangle from the x and y-axis bounds."
computeViewMessage **perform**.
^xyView

computeXYViewFromAxes
"Used to compute a default view rectangle from the x and y-axis bounds."
self
    computeXYViewFromxView: (
        self **xAxis leftBottom x** @ self **xAxis rightTop x**)
    yView: (self **yAxis leftBottom y** @ self **yAxis rightTop y**)

computeXYViewFromxView: xRangePoint **yView**: yRangePoint
"The user supplied range data is used to construct a rectangle denoting the plotting area. The view constructed is a rectangle in which all points are in user coordinates with x increasing to the right and y increasing upward. Additional space is reserved for the tick mark labels and a bit of extra white space."

```
| left bottom |
left := self yTicks size = 0
    ifTrue: [10]
    ifFalse: [
        20 + (self yTicks inject: 0 into: [:size :value |
            size max: (pane pen stringWidthOf: value printString)])].
bottom := self xTicks size = 0
    ifTrue: [10]
    ifFalse: [20 + pane pen font height].
self
    computeXYViewFromxView: xRangePoint xIndents: left@10
    yView: yRangePoint yIndents: 10@bottom
```

```
computeXYViewFromxView: xRangePoint xIndents: xIndents
yView: yRangePoint yIndents: yIndents
    "The user supplied range data is used to construct a rectangle denoting the plotting
    area. The view constructed is a rectangle with points in user coordinates with x
    increasing to the right and y increasing upward (left bottom is minimum x and y
    whereas the right top is maximum x and y). The x-indent is a point left@right; e.g.,
    5@10 specifies that an extra 5 pixels of space is needed on the left and 10 on the
    right. Similarly, the y-indent is a point top@bottom specifying space above
    and below. "
    | scale leftBottom rightTop leftBottomDelta rightTopDelta |

    "Determine boundaries of view without indents."
    leftBottom := xRangePoint x @ yRangePoint x.
    rightTop := xRangePoint y @ yRangePoint y.

    "Convert the indents in pane coordinates to user coordinates (the transformation is
    not yet available)."
    scale := (rightTop - leftBottom) / pane rectangle extent.
    leftBottomDelta := xIndents x@yIndents y.
    rightTopDelta := xIndents y@yIndents x.

    xyView :=
        Rectangle
            leftBottom: leftBottom - (leftBottomDelta * scale)
            rightTop: rightTop + (rightTopDelta * scale)

xView: xRangePoint xIndents: xIndents yView: yRangePoint yIndents: yIndents
    "The user supplied range data is used to construct a rectangle denoting the plotting
    area. The view constructed is a rectangle with points in user coordinates with x
    increasing to the right and y increasing upward (left bottom is minimum x and y
    whereas the right top is maximum x and y). The x-indent is a point left@right; e.g.,
    5@10 specifies that an extra 5 pixels of space is needed on the left and 10 on the
    right. Similarly, the y-indent is a point top@bottom specifying space above and
    below. "

    computeViewMessage := Message new
        receiver: self
        selector: #computeXYViewFromxView:xIndents:yView:yIndents:
        arguments: (Array
            with: xRangePoint
            with: xIndents
            with: yRangePoint
            with: yIndents)
```

```
xView: xRangePoint yView: yRangePoint
    "The user supplied range data is used to construct a rectangle denoting the plotting
    area. The view constructed is a rectangle in which all points are in user coordinates
    with x increasing to the right and y increasing upward. Additional space is
    reserved for the tick mark labels and a bit of extra white space."
    computeViewMessage := Message new
        receiver: self
        selector: #computeXYViewFromxView:yView:
        arguments: (Array
            with: xRangePoint
            with: yRangePoint)

xyView
    "Returns the rectangle denoting the plotting area. Compute it if not user supplied."
    xyView isNil ifTrue: [self computeXYView].
    ^xyView

displaying

transform: aPoint
    "Transform the point in user coordinates (with x increasing to the right and y
    increasing upward) to display coordinates."
    ^transformation transform: aPoint

plot
    "To plot, the user must provide a screen area for the window to be opened."
    | aWindow |
    aWindow := ViewManager new
        labelWithoutPrefix: self label;
        addSubpane: (pane := GraphPane new
            owner: self;
            style: GraphPane noScrollBarsFrameStyle;
            when: #getContents perform: #displayOn:;
            framingRatio: (0 @ 0 extent: 1 @ 1);
            stretch: 2;
            "0 => no scaling; 1 => scale maintaining aspect ratio; 2 => arbitrary scale"
            yourself).
    aWindow openIn: Display rectangleFromUser

displayOn: aPane
    "Display the axes and data points."
    transformation := Transformation from: self xyView to: aPane rectangle.
    aPane pen
        deleteAllSegments;
        erase;
        drawRetainPicture: [
            self displayAxesOn: aPane; displayPointsOn: aPane]
```

```
displayAxesOn: aPane
    "Displays the axes, the tick marks, and the values associated with the tick marks."
    | yExtent xExtent aPen xText yText |
    aPen := aPane pen. aPen setBackMode: Transparent.

    "The x-axis."
    aPen place: (self transform: self xAxis leftBottom).
    aPen goto: (self transform: self xAxis rightTop).

    self xTicksDo: [:transformedPoint :userPoint |
        xText := userPoint x printString.
        xExtent := (aPen stringWidthOf: xText) @ (aPen font height).
        aPen place: (transformedPoint up: 5); goto: (transformedPoint down: 5).
        aPen
            displayText: xText
            at: (transformedPoint leftAndDown: (xExtent x //2)@(xExtent y + 10))].

    "The y-axis."
    aPen place: (self transform: self yAxis leftBottom).
    aPen goto: (self transform: self yAxis rightTop).
    self yTicksDo: [:transformedPoint :userPoint |
        yText := userPoint y printString.
        yExtent := (aPen stringWidthOf: yText) @ (aPen font height).
        aPen place: (transformedPoint left: 5); goto: (transformedPoint right: 5).
        aPen
            displayText: yText
            at: (transformedPoint leftAndDown: (10+yExtent x)@(yExtent y // 3))]

displayPointsOn: aPane
    "Displays the data points with interconnecting line segments. Each line (set of
    segments) is plotted in the same area and distinguished by using the markers as
    points. A marker is a single character that can be specified by the user."
    | oldLocation aPen dot |
    aPen := aPane pen.
    aPen setTextAlign: TaCenter.
    self
        pointsDoFirst: [:point :marker |
            dot := (String with: marker).
            aPen displayText: dot at: (point leftAndUp: (0@5)); place: point]
        rest: [:point :marker |
            dot := (String with: marker).
            oldLocation := aPen location.
            aPen
                displayText: dot at: (point leftAndUp: (0@5));
                place: oldLocation; goto: point]
```

sequencing

```
xTicksDo: aBlock
    "Permits use in the form aLinePlot xTicksDo: [:transformedPoint :userPoint | ...]."
    | y |
    y := self xAxis top.
    self xTicks do: [:x | aBlock value: (self transform: x@y) value: x@y]

yTicksDo: aBlock
    "Permits use in the form aLinePlot yTicksDo: [:transformedPoint :userPoint | ...]."
    | x aPoint |
    x := self yAxis left.
    self yTicks do: [:y | aBlock value: (self transform: x@y) value: x@y]

originalPointsDoFirst: block1 rest: block2
    "Permits use in the form aLinePlot originalPointsDoFirst: [:point :marker | ...] rest:
    [:point :marker | ....]. A marker is a line labelling character."
    self pointCollectionsDo: [:pointCollection :marker |
        block1 value: pointCollection first value: marker.
        2 to: pointCollection size do: [:index |
            block2 value: (pointCollection at: index) value: marker]]

pointCollectionsDo: aBinaryBlock
    "Permits use in the form aLinePlot pointCollectionsDo: [:pointCollection :marker |
    ...]. A marker is a line labelling character."
    pointCollections with: markers do: [:pointCollection :marker |
        aBinaryBlock value: pointCollection value: marker]

pointsDoFirst: block1 rest: block2
    "Permits use in the form aLinePlot pointsDoFirst: [:point :marker | ...] rest: [:point
    :marker | ....]. A marker is a line labelling character."
    self pointCollectionsDo: [:pointCollection :marker |
        block1 value: (self transform: pointCollection first) value: marker.
        2 to: pointCollection size do: [:index | block2
            value: (self transform: (pointCollection at: index) value: marker]]
```

adding plots

```
add: xCollection and: yCollection marker: aCharacter
    "This method is used to add lines to the line plot."
    | points |
    points := OrderedCollection new.
    xCollection with: yCollection do: [:x :y | points add: x@y].
    pointCollections add: points asArray.
    markers add: aCharacter

add: points marker: aCharacter
    "This method is used to add lines to the line plot."
    pointCollections add: points.
    markers add: aCharacter
```

9.4 Conclusions

In this chapter, we showed how A.I. data types can be easily supported in Smalltalk and how Smalltalk's graphics capabilities can be used to advantage. More specifically, we introduced a FuzzySet class which inherits from Dictionary. We didn't argue that this was the best design but it was certainly the easiest and fastest to implement. We also introduced a number of classes for displaying simple line plots. In particular, the Transformation class supports a relatively general approach to mapping user coordinates to domain coordinates even when the coordinate systems are inverted.

Although we used it for a specific application, the plotting facility that we developed is relatively general purpose. More needs to be done to make it truly useful but this initial implementation can serve as a foundation for a more comprehensive facility.

9.5 References

1. Schmucker, Kurt J., Fuzzy Sets, Natural Language Computations, and Risk Analysis, Computer Science Press, Rockville, Maryland, 1984.

2. Zadeh, L., Knowledge Evaluation: Observations and Computation for Intelligent Control, Proceedings of the IEEE International Symposium on Intelligent Control, Philadelphia, Penn., 1987, pp. 302-308.

3. Lakoff, G., Hedges: Study in Meaning Criteria and the Logic of Fuzzy Concepts, Journal of Philosophical Logic, Vol. 2, 1973, pp. 458-508.

10

Dynamic Data Exchange

10.1 Introduction

Operating systems such as OS/2, Windows, and System 7 on the Macintosh now provide techniques for passing information between applications: **interapplication communication** (IAC) on the Mac and **dynamic data exchange** (DDE) [1] and **object linking and embedding** (OLE) for Windows. Such facilities are designed to permit integrated communities of applications to work together on a common problem; e.g., by connecting a spreadsheet to a word processor so that changes in the spreadsheet are reflected immediately (and automatically) in the text document. Other useful applications of this technique might include

- a display application linked to a communications application connected to a remote information network providing real-time data on subjects such as the stock market, weather forecasts, airline schedules, sports standings,
- a business application querying an SQL database manager for payroll information.

In this chapter, we will focus exclusively on DDE. DDE is most appropriate in situations that don't involve explicit user control. In the first example, the display automatically changes when the remote information changes. In the second, the SQL manager is queried by the business application (perhaps indirectly) as a consequence of user interaction in the application interface.

Note that we can't take advantage of DDE unless the applications have been specifically designed to support it. This is the case, for example, with Microsoft products like Word and Excel along with Digitalk's Smalltalk/V for Windows and OS/2.

To provide a flavor for the facility, we will briefly review some of the DDE features provided by Smalltalk/V and use it in a simple example.

10.2 Conversations Through Clients and Servers

When two applications are communicating, they are said to be participating in a DDE **conversation.** One application plays the role of a **client**, and the other a **server**. A conversation is initiated by the client application. The server application responds to the client. A server may have many clients. Moreover, at any one time, an application can be engaged in several conversations at once either as a client, a server, or both. Once a conversation is initiated, applications can exchange data in various ways, including:

- the client requesting data from the server,
- the client requesting that it be informed whenever a specified data item changes (but without being sent new data); this is termed a **warm link**,
- the client requesting that it be provided with new data whenever a specified data item changes; this is termed a **hot link**,
- the client requesting that the server execute a specific command.

Information passed between clients and servers is identified by a three level name: (1) an **application name**, (2) a **topic name**, and (3) an **item name**. The first two uniquely identify a DDE conversation. The third permits distinct data items to be passed as part of the conversation specified by the first two parameters.

10.3 A Simple Form Letter System

Consider a system (written in Smalltalk) that permits a secretary to create form letters from information stored in a database. Access to the database could be provided through a simple user interface that permits the secretary to both view and modify the database records. To print the information, the secretary would choose one or more form letters as the repository for the information and request a printout.

Although it is possible to create crude text documents with Smalltalk, it clearly is not the ideal tool for this job. A much better tool for that task is a document processing system like Microsoft Word. What we would like to be able to do is use DDE to harness Word for the task. To achieve this, we need to do two things:

- Use Word to create hot-linkable form letters.
- Develop a Smalltalk application to provide data for the form letters.

For illustration purposes, we will create two form letters (see Figures 10.1 and 10.2) and provide a prototype Smalltalk application (see Figure 10.3)

Figure 10.1 — Form letter 1.

that allows a secretary to enter information and print it on the form letters. One of the printed form letters is shown in Figure 10.4.

Figure 10.2 — Form letter 2.

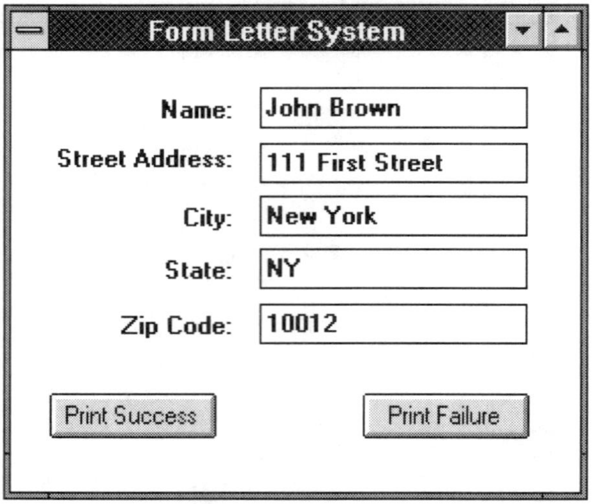

Figure 10.3 — Smalltalk user interface for the form letter system.

Figure 10.4 — A completed form letter.

In a complete application, the user interface would additionally permit the secretary to choose among different form letters, and allow manipulation of actual records in a database. The database details will be ignored to permit us to focus on the DDE aspects of the application.

10.4 Creating the Form Letters

From the point of view of a hot linked document, the two Microsoft Word documents are the clients and the Smalltalk application is the server. In this scenario, the conversations are initiated by the Word documents. Each document asks the Smalltalk application to provide it with new data any time in the future when the values of hot linked fields are changed.

To create a hot linked form letter, one or more fields must be connected with a hot link. To create such a hot linked field, Word requires a running server that is willing to respond to the specified application name and topic. Consequently, the Smalltalk application has to be developed first and must actually be running before the form letters can be created.

Actually creating a form letter is quite simple. First, write the form letter without hot linked fields. Next, for each hot linked field, choose **Field** from the **Insert** menu, select any field type like **Link** (see Figure 10.5) from the list of field types, and fill in the entry field with "**ddeauto** application name, topic name, and item name". To create a warm link rather than a hot link, type **dde** rather than **ddeauto**.

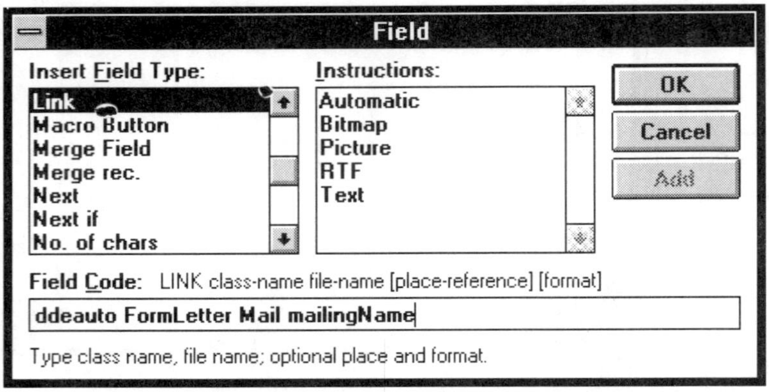

Figure 10.5 — Inserting a hot linked field into Word.

Word automatically inserts the special braces that you see in Figures 10.1 and 10.2 and asks all existing servers if any can service application "FormLetter" and topic "Mail". If none can, an warning is generated.

Once all hot linked fields have been created, the document can be saved in the normal way. When a hot linked document is opened in the future, Word will prompt the user as shown in Figure 10.6 to determine whether or not to set up the links. If the user replies with **Yes**, connection is attempted. If the FormLetter application is running, the link will be successful.

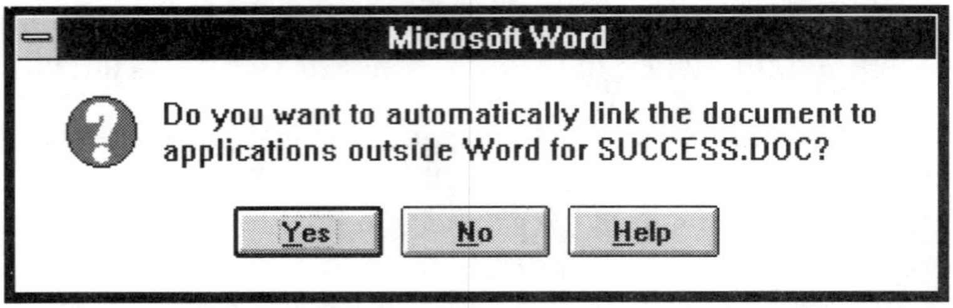

Figure 10.6 — The confirm dialog for establishing the links.

10.5 Designing the Form Letter System

The system that we want to implement is complicated by the fact that we want the Smalltalk application and Word to be able to play two roles; i.e., for each one to be a server in one context and a client in another. More specifically, we will first start Word running without opening any files and then we will start the Smalltalk application. We would like to have the Smalltalk application in control.

To achieve this we will introduce two channels (see Figure 10.7): a command channel and a data channel. The **command channel** will be used by the Smalltalk application to issue "execute command" requests to Word (our Smalltalk application will be playing the role of a client). The **data channel** will provide Word with new field information when such information becomes available (our Smalltalk application in this case will be a server that services requests for its hot linked data).

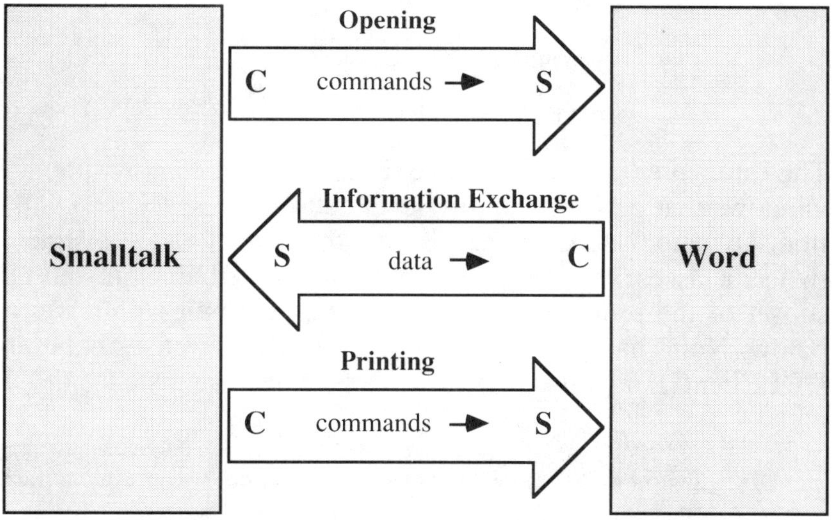

Figure 10.7 — The client (C) versus the server (S).

The command channel needs to be used in two different contexts: first to cause Word to open form letter documents needed by our application and second to cause Word to print the contents of one of these documents.

The data channel is needed to pass up-to-date field information every time a form letter is to be printed; e.g., by clicking on **Print Success** or **Print Failure** buttons. At that point, all field values are exported through the data channel to update the Word document.

The operations to be implemented will follow the sequence: open the application, update hot linked fields, print the document. This sequence, along with the corresponding channels, was summarized in Figure 10.7.

10.6 DDE Support in Smalltalk/V

Smalltalk/V for Windows and OS/2 provides support for dynamic data exchange through six classes organized as follows:

```
Object
    DynamicDataExchange
        DDEClient
        DDEServer
    Window
        DDEAuxWindow
            DDEAuxClient
            DDEAuxServer
```

The three auxiliary window classes are private classes supporting invisible windows that perform the low-level details necessary for DDE communication. DynamicDataExchange is best thought of as an abstract class for the two subclasses which are for public use; i.e., DDEClient and DDEServer. A subset of the protocol necessary for our example application is described below. Note that if we wish to be a client, we must obtain an instance of DDEClient. If we wish to be a server, we need an instance of DDEServer.

client protocol

DDEClient **newClient**: aViewManager **application**: serverName **topic**: aString

- To create a channel (for a client) to communicate with a server. The server name is a string.

aDDEClient **executeCommand**: aString

- (For a client) to request a server to execute a command it understands.

server protocol

DDEServer **newServer**: aViewManager **application**: serverName **topic**: aString

- To create a channel (for a server) to communicate with a client. The server name is a string.

aDDEServer **addExportedItem**: aString **object**: aStringOrAnInteger

- (For a server) to indicate to a client that aString is the item name that it will provide data for and that aStringOrAnInteger is the initial value.

aDDEServer **updateExportedItem**: aString **object**: aStringOrAnInteger

- As above but updates the client with a new value.

common protocol

aDynamicDataExchange **terminate**

- To end a conversation.

10.7 Implementing the Form Letter System

In this prototype, method **open** sets up a simple form filling user interface — this method was constructed with the window builder. This interface consists of static text panes, non-static text panes and two print buttons. The #opened event handler invokes method **initializeChannels** to create both an instance of DDEClient (commandChannel) and an instance of DDEServer (dataChannel) to set up a communication link.

The server DDE instance (dataChannel) is created with application name 'FormLetter' and topic 'Mail' and is provided with the list of data items that it can supply to its clients; specifically, 'mailingName', 'mailingStreetAddress', 'mailingCity', 'mailingState' and 'mailingZipCode'. The string 'unknown' is provided as the initial value for each data item. Once this is done, our application can behave as a server to any client requesting hot or warm linked data items with those names. The server does not need to distinguish between hot or warm links — the distinction is handled by the client. The server assumes it is working with a client using hot links. The DDE server instance holds the latest information supplied until it is revised. This way, new clients can link up and have access to the latest information or old clients can request the most up-to-date explicitly if it uses warm links. One nice thing about the DDE links is that data item requests by clients need not involve user intervention. It's all handled by the lower levels of the system.

The client DDE instance (commandChannel) needs to set up a conversation link with Word in order to be able to issue commands. Because the link is with a vendor specific product, technical documentation is essential for this to work. In our case, we used Microsoft Word for Windows [2] as our source of information. It turns out that Word will respond to user commands written in WordBASIC (the language is covered in detail in the documentation) if the link is set up with application name 'WinWord' and topic 'System'. As can be seen from actual use of the **executeCommand**: message, Word commands are enclosed in square brackets. This is detailed in Listing 10.1; e.g., in the last few lines of method **initializeChannels** and in method **printFile**:.

At open time, our application uses the built-in file dialog to ask the user to locate two form letters — for our demonstration, we specify "SUCCESS.DOC" and "FAILURE.DOC". Commands are then issued to Word to open these two files. When the commands are executed, the Word application window begins to flash and continues doing so until the mouse is clicked in the window. At this point, the user is prompted (by Word) to determine if the document should be automatically linked to the form letter application (see Figure 10.6) — remember, the form letters were created and stored with all of the necessary hot link information necessary for re-establishing the links. The user should respond in the affirmative. Note that the dataChannel must have been created and properly initialized at this time because Word will actually broadcast a query to all active applications to see if there exists one willing to service it under the 'FormLetter/Mail' application/topic name. Our Smalltalk application acknowledges its ability to service the request and the link is established. Note: Acknowledgments are actually performed automatically and transparently by the dataChannel (the server DDE instance) — this is part of the low-level protocol that users don't have to worry about when using the DDE facility in Smalltalk. This would not be the case, for example, if DDE were implemented by the user in some other language; e.g., C.

Normally, the user enters information in the form letter application (see Figure 10.3) and then clicks on either the **Print Success** or **Print Failure** button. The corresponding #clicked handlers are methods **printSuccess**: and **printFailure**: which cause method **updateExportFields** to export the contents of the entry fields to Word via the data channel. Finally, the appropriate Word Basic commands are sent through the command channel to cause Word to print the appropriate form letter.

Ultimately, when our application window is closed, the two DDE channels should be terminated. In our close event handler (method **close**:) we use method **terminateChannels** which asks Word to close both form letter documents, and then terminates both commandChannel and dataChannel. Message **close** then closes our application window.

Listing 10.1 — Class FormLetterSystem.

class	FormLetterSystem
superclass	ViewManager
instance variables	fields successName failureName dataChannel commandChannel

class methods

examples

```
example1
    "FormLetterSystem example1"
    self new open
```

WindowBuilder compatibility

```
wbCreated
    ^true
```

instance methods

DDE client updating

```
updateExportFields
    "Update the contents of the fields for the DDE Clients."
    fields associationsDo: [:pair |
        "pair is (entryFieldName->entryField)"
        dataChannel
            updateExportedItem: pair key
            object: pair value contents trimBlanks]
```

printing

```
printFile: aFilename
    "Update all panes so that the most up to data information is printed and then print
    the form letter in aFilename."
    self updateExportFields.
    commandChannel
        executeCommand: '[Activate "', aFilename, '"]';
        executeCommand: '[FilePrint ()]'

printSuccess: aPane
    self printFile: successName

printFailure: aPane
    self printFile: failureName
```

starting a new application

```
open
    "*** Code not shown ***"

opened: aPane
    "The #opened event handler for the application."
    | result |
    "Set up the EntryField panes in the fields collection."
    fields := Dictionary new
        at: 'mailingName' put: (self paneNamed: 'nameField');
        at: 'mailingStreetAddress' put: (self paneNamed: 'streetField');
        at: 'mailingCity' put: (self paneNamed: 'cityField');
        at: 'mailingState' put: (self paneNamed: 'stateField');
        at: 'mailingZipCode' put: (self paneNamed: 'zipField');
        yourself.
    fields do: [:aField | aField contents: ''].
    (self paneNamed: 'nameField') setFocus.
    "Try to open the DDE channels."
    self initializeChannels ifFalse: [^self close]

initializeChannels
    successName := (FileDialog new openFile: 'Pick Success Letter') file.
    (successName isNil or: [successName isEmpty])
        ifTrue: [^false].
    failureName := (FileDialog new openFile: 'Pick Failure Letter') file.
    (failureName isNil or: [failureName isEmpty])
        ifTrue: [^false].
    dataChannel := DDEServer
        newServer: self
        application: 'FormLetter'
        topic: 'Mail'.
```

```
    dataChannel isNil
        ifTrue: [self error: 'Form letter system DDE error']
        ifFalse: [
            dataChannel
                addExportedItem: 'mailingName' object: 'unknown';
                addExportedItem: 'mailingStreetAddress' object: 'unknown';
                addExportedItem: 'mailingCity' object: 'unknown';
                addExportedItem: 'mailingState' object: 'unknown';
                addExportedItem: 'mailingZipCode' object: 'unknown'].
    "Determine if Word is already running. If not, make it run."
    (KernelLibrary getModuleHandle: 'WinWord.exe') = 0   "not running"
        ifTrue: [KernelLibrary winExec: 'WinWord.exe' cmdShow: SwShow].
    commandChannel := DDEClient
        newClient: self
        application: 'WinWord'
        topic: 'System'.
    commandChannel isNil
        ifTrue: [self terminateChannels; error: 'Word not responding'].
    commandChannel
        executeCommand:
            '[if AppMinimize() then AppRestore] ',
            '[FileOpen ("', successName, '")] ',
            '[FileOpen ("', failureName, '")]'.
    ^true
```

ending the application (window event processing)

```
terminateChannels
    commandChannel notNil
        ifTrue: [
            commandChannel canExecuteCommand
                ifTrue: [commandChannel
                    executeCommand: '[Activate "', successName, '",1]';
                    executeCommand: '[FileClose ()]';
                    executeCommand: '[Activate "', failureName, '",1]';
                    executeCommand: '[FileClose ()]' ].
            commandChannel terminate].
    dataChannel notNil
        ifTrue: [dataChannel terminate]

close: aPane
    "Close the receiver."
    self terminateChannels.
    ^self close
```

10.8 Using Warm Instead of Hot Links

Using warm links instead of hot links is merely a matter of creating the form letter fields in Word using field type **dde** instead of **ddeauto** (recall Figure 10.5). However, now the fields in Word are updated only on request. More specifically, the user can select menu item **Links ...** from the **Edit** menu. A dialog box (see Figure 10.8) appears that permits multiple entries in a list pane to be selected and updated by clicking on the **Update Now** button. It is also possible to change a hot link (shown as **automatic**) to a warm link (shown as **manual**). Note that no change is required in our Smalltalk application.

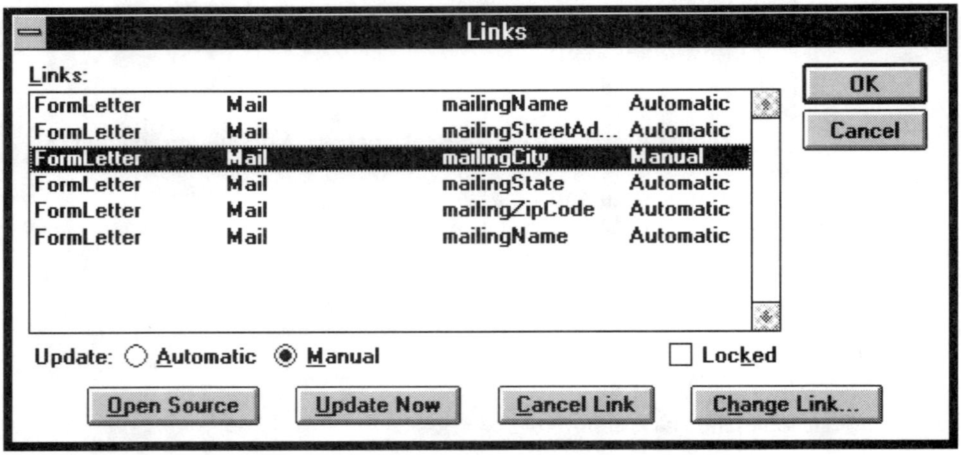

Figure 10.8 — Updating warm links.

On the other hand, if our Smalltalk application were a client, additional protocol that we haven't discussed would have to be used; e.g., protocol to establish hot and warm links, to request data for a warm link and to terminate both kinds of links. The protocol for establishing hot and warm links would also specify which application method to execute when the client receives new items.

10.9 Conclusions

The DDE facility provided in Digitalk's Smalltalk/V for Windows (or OS/2) provides a powerful protocol for establishing conversations between independently executing applications. As shown in our example application, the provided client and server classes successfully shield the programmer from many tedious low-level details.

With the expectation that more and more applications will provide support for DDE (or OLE), greater opportunity for coupling the functionality of diverse products will arise.

10.10 Acknowledgments

This chapter owes a great deal to Jon Hylands for helping us explore and develop the DDE facilities, to the Microsoft Windows reference manuals which contain a clear exposition of DDEs, and to the examples incorporated with the Smalltalk/V for Windows (in particular, an example permitting Smalltalk expressions to be executed from Word and another linking a graphical dashboard application to Excel).

10.11 References

1. Microsoft Windows Guide to Programming, Version 3, Microsoft Press, 1990.

2. Microsoft Word For Windows and OS/2 Technical Reference, Microsoft Press, 1990.

Index

A

Account manager 81, 84, 92
Animation 47

B

Bitmaps 34, 47, 48, 49, 50, 55, 56, 60, 104, 111

C

Classes
  AccountManager 86, 87
  BinaryTree 1, 4, 10
  Bitmap 111
  Dictionary 112
  DiskObject 39
  EmptyBinaryTree 10, 12
  FilmLoop 51
  FormLetterSystem 179
  FuzzySet 144, 153
  LanguageTranslator 75
  LinePlot 153, 159, 160
  ListExtensionDialog 110
  ListQueryDialog 107
  Message 36, 37, 45
  NonEmptyBinaryTree 10, 14
  PictureViewer 114
  TicTacToeGame 124
  TicTacToeWindow 130, 135, 136
  TilingPane 121, 130, 133
  Transformation 158
  Trie 21, 23, 25, 27, 31
Clients 170, 175
Conversations 170

D

Dialog windows 62
Disk bitmaps 33, 35
Disk objects 33, 39, 42, 56, 60
Dynamic data exchange 169, 176
Dynamic representations 45

E

Encapsulators 33, 46
Event handler 65, 70, 121
Event-driven framework 61, 80
Events 122

F

Film loops 47, 50, 55
Flicker 59, 60

Form letter application 171, 173, 175
Fuzzy sets 141, 142, 143, 167
Fuzzy set operations 144, 147
Fuzzy set quantifiers 151

G

Generalization 19, 30, 31, 32

H

Hot links 170, 182

I

Indirection objects 43, 44
Interapplication communication 169

L

Language translation 73
Line plots 143, 153, 167

M

Meta-level facilities 33
doesNotUnderstand 36, 37, 44, 45
perform 36
Modal windows 108
Model-pane-dispatcher 61
Model-view-controller 61
Monitoring 46
Multiple representations 1,33

O

Object filer 39
Object linking and embedding 169
Object mutation 11, 33
become 12, 36, 38, 42, 43, 45
Object tables 43
Operating system events 121, 122, 139
Owners 64

P

Panes 67
Picture viewer 104, 105, 106, 113
Pluggable panes 130

R

Remote objects 46
Reuse 19

S

Scroll bars 99
Servers 170, 175
Sharable dictionary 26
Smalltalk window events 62, 64, 65, 80, 121, 139
Specialization 26
Species 112
Streams 16

T

Tiling panes 129, 130, 139
Transactions 82
Transformations 155
Tansparent forwarding 33
Trees 1
  empty binary trees 1, 3, 9, 10
  non-empty binary trees 1, 3, 9, 10, 13
Tries 20, 21, 24
  compressed tries 32
  digital tries 20

U

Updating panes
  change/update mechanism 71, 72
  direct messaging 71, 72

V

Validation 94, 95, 96, 97
  intrusive feedback 96
  unobtrusive feedback 96
View managers 62
Viewpoint
  implementor 25, 112
  user 25, 112

W

Warm links 170, 182
Window builder 83, 85, 86, 102
Window lifecycle 90